HIS FIRST **50** YEARS

CHARLES PHILLIPS

ARTABRAS · NEW YORK LONDON PARIS

EDITOR, ABBEVILLE PRESS: Alan Axelrod
PROJECT EDITOR, ARCHIE COMIC PUBLICATIONS, INC.: Donna Block
DESIGNER: Patricia Fabricant
PRODUCTION EDITOR: Cristine Mesch
PRODUCTION SUPERVISOR: Hope Koturo
RESEARCH ASSISTANT, ARCHIE COMIC PUBLICATIONS, INC.: Paul Castiglia

Photography by Steven Begleiter

Printed and bound in Italy.

First edition, second printing.

Library of Congress Cataloging-in-Publication Data

Phillips, Charles.
Archie : his first 50 years / Charles Phillips. — 1st ed.
p.   cm.
ISBN 0-89660-035-1
1. Andrews, Archie (fictitious character) I. Goldwater, John L.
Archie. II. Title.
DS313.B39   1991
955.05'1 — dc20   91-16839

The Archie characters were created by John L. Goldwater.

Contents

A Boy Among Men

When Archie Andrews's first words ballooned into print during the winter of 1941, the world was at war and comic books had just become big business. The events were related.

Superman, whose very name echoes the Nietzschean claims of the Nazis, had only appeared in June 1938. A daydream of American power to answer the anxieties produced by Germany's conquest of Europe, the Man of Steel was the prototype for an entirely new kind of "strip." The amazingly enthusiastic reception accorded him triggered an explosion in the world of comics, raising comic books to startling heights of popularity.

According to Archie's creator, it was a deliberate attempt to produce a popular comic-book character who was the antithesis of Superman that led to the birth of Riverdale's favorite son, the gap-toothed, freckle-faced, slightly bemused teenager, who—in December of 1941, at least—wanted to be called "Chick" Andrews.

Cartooning, of course, has a long, if not venerable, pedigree. Histories of the comics often hark back to cave drawings as the first attempts at narrative art. Some have seen in the sublime Bayeux tapestry of A.D. 1150 a medieval French comic strip depicting the events that culminated in the Battle of Hastings. And it is true that the word *cartoon* originally denoted the outline drawings used as the basis for frescoes, mosaics, and tapestries. Until the mid-nineteenth century, satirical drawings were known as caricatures or hieroglyphics. In 1843, London's *Punch,* the first regular illustrated comic weekly, lambasted the "cartoon" designs for murals to adorn the walls of Parliament with satirical versions of its own. From that time on, *cartoon* came to mean any self-contained, single drawing, usually accompanied by a caption, title, or crude "word balloon." But it was not until the circulation battles of the late nineteenth century between Joseph Pulitzer's New York *World* and William Randolph Hearst's *Journal* that the cartoon began to develop into the comic strip. The brightly colored nightshirt of R. F. Outcault's slum-dwelling Yellow Kid became visual shorthand for the sensationalist, circulation-driven journalism practiced by Hearst and Pulitzer. As the Kid lost

HERE Y'ARE, GANG, AMERICA'S NEWEST BOY FRIEND, ARCHIE ANDREWS, CHRISTENED ARCHIBALD. HE HATES ARCHIE, SO IF YOU VALUE LIFE AND LIMB, CALL HIM "CHICK". RIGHT NOW HE'S RISKING LIFE AND LIMB TO IMPRESS HIS NEW NEIGHBOR— BETTY COOPER....

popularity to the solid middle-class she-nanigans of the Katzenjammers at the turn of the century, the comics developed into a separate and permanent part of the American newspaper.

Stand-alone collections of these comic strips, printed directly from newspaper plates, appeared even before World War I. At least one of them—*Mutt and Jeff,* which the Chicago *American* issued (naturally) as a circulation stunt—was quite successful. Though almost fifty thousand readers wrote in for copies of the book, the ever-conservative publishing industry ignored the phenomenon and continued to pump out popular fiction reprinted from pulp magazines and newspaper serials as mass-circulation entertainment.

In the late twenties, George Delacorte, who would one day publish Dell Comics, played around with a tabloid-format comic book containing original drawings rather than comic-strip reprints. The idea bombed. In the thirties, the Whitman Publishing Company experimented with a three-inch-square, two-inch-deep book that offered typeset continuous narrative on the left-hand page and one panel of a corresponding and continuing strip on the right-hand page. Called Big Little Books, they sold well—until, in fact, the comic book as we know it today killed them off.

Comic-book publishing got its real start in the mid-thirties when manufacturers offered anthologies of newspaper "funnies" as premiums for shoppers who bought their products. M. C. Gaines slapped a ten-cent price sticker on a bunch of copies of one such premium, *Famous Funnies,* and talked a few newsstand dealers into carrying them as a one-shot offering. They sold out immediately, and in 1933 George Delacorte agreed to publish thirty-five thousand of the premium anthologies and release them through chain stores. Again, the odd little publications sold out quickly.

Still, no one really thought comic books

could make it on their own. They were seen as a gimmick, a come-on for a general shopping tour, mere newspaper reprints that were not worth distributing through the ordinary magazine channels.

Then the New York *Daily Post* ran an advertisement in early 1934 thoughtfully promoting comics as a surefire draw for new readers, and a few pioneers began to see the possibilities of a market for comics themselves. Eastern Color Printing, the company that had produced most of the premium books, published the first comic book created specifically for newsstand sales. It, too, was called *Famous Funnies;* it, too, sold for ten cents; and it, too, consisted mostly of reprints, with a sprinkling of puzzles, magic tricks, and "oddity" cartoons patterned after Robert L. Ripley's syndicated newspaper feature *Believe It or Not.*

The first issue lost money, but the second was profitable enough to give Gaines heart. He published a third issue made up entirely of a vintage newspaper strip called *Skippy.* Then in 1935 he went on to produce for Delacorte a comic magazine called *Popular Comics.* In short order, the United Features Syndicate came out with *Tip Top Comics,* the McCay Company brought out *King Comics,* and the King Features Syndicate leased the rights (or, as we would say today, "licensed") all its strips for comic-book reprint. Playing off the popularity of tough-guy detective fiction, Gaines came out in 1937 with the first comic book to offer a strip dedicated to a specific genre, *Detective Comics.* A year later, *Action Comics* made its first appearance.

It was in *Action Comics* that Gaines saw the spot for a strange strip he had been interested in for some time. Two stubborn kids from Cleveland, Jerry Siegal and Joe Shuster, came up with the idea while they were still in high school. They had been trying for five years to sell their creation to the daily newspapers when Gaines offered them space for *Superman* in his new action-adventure comic book.

From the first panel of Archie's first appearance, Pep #22 (December 1941)

Within a few months, the circulation of *Action Comics* doubled. By spring 1939, *Superman Quarterly Magazine* hit the streets. Later that year, the strip was taken by McClure, a publishing syndicate created in the 1880s by S. S. McClure before he founded his famous magazine. In 1940, *Superman* became a hit radio program. The first *Superman* animated cartoon, produced by Max Fleischer and Paramount Studios, was released September 26, 1941. Not only *Superman,* but comic books in general were here to stay.

The first year after the Man of Steel's debut, a devotee could find 60 comic-book titles for sale. By the end of 1941, some 168 comic-book titles cluttered newsstands, candy stores, and Army PXs. If there were any doubt that *Superman* was behind the boom, all one had to do was look at the dozens of imitations that had sprung up. One of the best, *Captain Marvel,* so perfectly duplicated *Superman*'s appeal that National Periodical Publications, who owned the rights to Superman, sued Fawcett, the publishers of *Captain Marvel,* and won an injunction against the rival costumed crusader.

The early forties incarnated an entire pantheon of "superheroes," less clearly exact copies but no less clearly capitalizing on *Superman*'s popularity. What often was not at all clear was the identity of the publishers. Many titles popped up once, seemingly out of nowhere, sold out, then vanished for good. Even the established publishers of comics were more interested in volume than quality, and any given house would have several titles, each featuring its own superheroes.

One of the more active of the superhero mills was MLJ Comics, which had entered the comic-book field late in 1939, founded by Maurice Coyne (the "M"), Louis Silberkleit (the "L"), and John Goldwater (the "J"). Goldwater ran the editorial side of the operation, Silberkleit the publishing end, and Coyne kept the books. All three came from publishing backgrounds; Coyne had been an accountant with a

major publisher of technical magazines, Silberkleit a publisher of pulps, and Goldwater a reporter and editor for newspapers and such magazines as *Pictorial Review.*

Coyne and Silberkleit had met casually in the course of their work and decided to form a company. They called it Columbia Publishing, which became the major publisher of pulp magazines after Street and Smith. But, evidently, publishing was then, as now, not the most stable of professions, and all three men found themselves in the late thirties working for someone else—the same someone else. They decided to try their hand at comic books.

By 1941, MLJ had a large stable of strangely garbed, extremely patriotic strongmen: Steel Sterling ("the Man of Steel") in *Zip Comics,* the Black Hood ("the Man of Mystery") in *Top-Notch Comics,* the Shield in *Pep Comics,* and a host of others—the Comet, the Rocket, the Wizard, Mr. Justice, Bob Phantom, the Hangman. MLJ had its good-guy boxers, its detectives (Oriental and Occidental), its young adventurers, its American fighting men: Kay O. Ward and the St. Louis Kid; Fu Chang, International Detective, and Bently of Scotland Yard; Corporal Collins, Sergeant Boyle, and The Midshipman. There was even a masked defender of the First Amendment called the Press Guardian.

MLJ's action and adventure comics were not especially noteworthy. Looking through them today, the connection between the sudden love for superheroes and the nation's growing willingness to fight seems especially evident. There is much war hysteria in these hastily drawn, simply plotted adolescent daydreams. Beyond the standard hero fare, the characters are derivative of long-standing popular icons: a Joe Palooka from the daily strips, a Charlie Chan from fiction and film. But it was from radio, then in its heyday, that *Archie*'s creator would derive the inspiration for MLJ's most enduring and original character.

According to John Goldwater, he first got

the idea for a "normal" teenager from *Andy Hardy,* a very popular radio show (and later a movie series starring Mickey Rooney), and decided to call the strip *Archie* after a high school chum. The story goes that Goldwater then turned to the MLJ bullpen and asked all the young artists and writers there to try their hand at working up the strip. It was Bob Montana who came up with the image of Archie, a younger version of today's familiar seventeen-year-old, who—wavy-haired, bucktoothed, and knickers-clad—does indeed resemble Mickey Rooney with a bit of Tom Sawyer thrown in.

Teamed with writer Vic Bloom, under the strong editorial hand of a burly, ex-professional football player named Harry Shorten, Montana produced the first *Archie* story for *Pep Comics #22,* which appeared in December 1941. The comic book was the stomping ground of MLJ's prime superhero, the

Shield, and *Archie* was merely a supporting feature. Not all of the *Archie* cast appeared in that first story, only Betty, Jughead, Archie's parents, and young Mr. Andrews himself. Veronica would not arrive until April of the next year, Mr. Weatherbee later that spring, Miss Grundy and Reggie in the spring of 1942, and Mr. Lodge in the fall.

John Goldwater claims that he knew from the beginning the "normal" Archie would be as popular as the hypernormal Superman. Despite his prescience, it took the strip most of a year to develop its major characters and much longer to develop what most of us would recognize as its most basic—and everlastingly popular—situation, the triangular relationship among Betty, Archie, and Veronica. By late 1942, Montana's mythical Riverdale High stories had become so popular that MLJ commissioned him to draw a whole comic book devoted to Archie and his friends. *Archie #1* came out in the winter of that year, just as the artist entered the Army.

Wavy-haired, bucktoothed Bob Montana was born in Stockton, California, in 1920, the son of a vaudeville banjoist named Ray Coleman, who called himself the Great Montana, and a Ziegfeld girl named Roberta Pandolfini, who went by the stage name of Bobby Gerald. By the time young Robert and his sister, Ruth, had

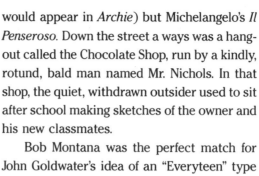

Bob Montana

joined the act, doing rope tricks and singing harmony, the family had legally changed its name to Montana. At six, Bob was already sketching cartoons backstage during the Montanas' cross-country tours.

In 1930, with vaudeville dead, the family moved to a farm in New Hampshire and opened a restaurant, both of which they lost to the Depression in 1932. From a hotel room in Boston, the Montanas launched another restaurant, the Ranchero, which, after the repeal of Prohibition, became enormously popular. Fresh from Exeter Art School in Back Bay, then the School of the Museum of Fine Arts in Boston, the thirteen-year-old Montana went from table to table sketching caricatures.

In 1935, Montana's father died suddenly of a heart attack. A year later his mother married a customer she had met at the restaurant, closed down the Ranchero, and moved the kids with her to a house in Haverhill, Massachusetts. There Montana would spend what he later called the three best years of his life, at Haverhill High. In front of the school sat a bronze replica of *The Thinker,* not Rodin's (as would appear in *Archie*) but Michelangelo's *Il Penseroso.* Down the street a ways was a hangout called the Chocolate Shop, run by a kindly, rotund, bald man named Mr. Nichols. In that shop, the quiet, withdrawn outsider used to sit after school making sketches of the owner and his new classmates.

Bob Montana was the perfect match for John Goldwater's idea of an "Everyteen" type patterned after Andy Hardy. After the war, in 1946, Montana returned to take charge of producing *Archie* as a daily newspaper strip, continuing to draw it until his own sudden death—like his father, he was the victim of a heart attack—in 1975. A rootless child who loved his high school years, Montana gave more than the statue of *The Thinker,* the hometown soda shop, and a number of his teenage pals to Riverdale. He gave the strip the emotional strength of his own nostalgia to create an idealized picture of teenage life that we all recognize, but none of us quite lived.

The Thinker, by Rodin via Montana

Young Archie Andrews made his first appearance in December 1941. The character, created by John L. Goldwater, and the story, by MLJ Comics' stable artist Bob Montana, were supporting features of Pep #22, a comic book that featured a superhero called The Shield. Accompanying Archie on that first outing were Jughead, whose real name would one day be Forsythe P. Jones; the pubescent Betty Cooper; and Archie's hapless parents.

HE FLIES THROUGH THE AIR.. WITH THE GREATEST OF EASE, ARCHIE SHOULD'VE STUCK TO THE FLYING TRAPEZE.

HERE, SON, HERE.. MOTHER'S READY TO CATCH YOU!

HAPPY, STICKY LANDINGS!

TAFFY

ARCHIE'S FOOT CONNECTS WITH THE CONTROL LEVER, AND..

OOWW! TAFFY!

STOP THAT MACHINE! STOP IT!

GLUB, GLUB.. JUSH WAIT'LL I GET HOLD OF THAT CLUMSY KID!!

LOOK-CLOSELY AND.. YOU'LL RECOGNIZE J.B. COOPER, BETTY'S FATHER!

BUT MR. COOPER, I CAN EXPLAIN!

YOU STOP AND EXPLAIN. I'LL KEEP ON GOING!

TAFFY! PHOOEY!

GIRLS! DOUBLE PHOOEY!

SOME KID, THAT ARCHIE, HUH GANG? THERE'S ANOTHER BARREL OF TROUBLE.. AND FUN WAITING FOR HIM AND HIS PAL, JUGHEAD, IN. THE NEXT ISSUE OF PEP COMICS! IF YOUR HEART IS WEAK AND YOU CAN'T STAND LAUGHING TOO MUCH THEN DON'T READ IT— BECAUSE YOU'LL ROAR UNTIL YOU CAN'T CATCH YOUR BREATH AND THE TEARS WILL ROLL. ARCHIE, COMIC'S LAUGH SENSATION!

The first of three accounts of Veronica Lodge's arrival in River-dale appeared in the April 1942 issue of Pep #26.

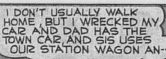

WHAT'S THE IDEA GOIN' HOME WITH THAT TUX! THE OTHER BUS-BOY NEEDS IT. NOW TAKE IT OFF!!

AW GEE, BOSS! I HAVEN'T GOT ANY OTHER CLOTHES!! AND I'VE GOT MY GIRL HERE!

SOMEBODY'S GOT TO TAKE THESE DISHES OUT!! NOW YOU CAN EITHER TAKE THAT TUX OFF OR WORK.

I'LL WORK. WAIT'LL I EXPLAIN!

COME ON, VERONICA, LET'S DANCE.

OH ARCHIE, YOU DANCE DIVINELY.

JIGGERS, THE BOSS!! I GOTTA DO SOMETHIN'

MEET PENNY REEMS, VERONICA HERE'S THAT DANCE I PROMISED YOU, PENN!

WISH I COULD REMEMBER WHERE I MET THAT CHARACTER.

PHEW! THEY DIDN'T SEE ME! TWO MORE LOADS AND I CAN REST!

(PUFF) JUST GOT BACK IN TIME!

RIGHT HERE, WAITER! WE'RE READY TO TO ORDER.

DID YOU SAY AVOCADO CRABMEAT, VERONICA!

OH MY GOSH! THAT'S $5 A PLATE AN I HAVE ONLY $7.25 LEFT OF MY $12 SALARY!

I'D BETTER GIVE THE ORDER TO PIERRE, THE CHEF, MYSELF SO IT WILL BE JUST RIGHT!

GOODNESS ARCHIE! DO YOU KNOW THE CHEF TOO?

WHAT A SPOT!--- ENTERTAINING A SUB-DEB, AN' BEIN' A BUS-BOY AT THE SAME TIME!

Veronica's father made his debut in 1942 as Burton K. Lodge in the Pep *#31 story.*

OPPOSITE, TOP TO BOTTOM: Splash panel from "Camera Bugs," Pep #48; from Archie's debut in Pep #22; splash panel from "Prom Pranks," Archie #1

ne of the secrets to Archie's success is the unvarying character traits of the stories' personalities. Their concerns, their possessions, the cut of their clothes, and the architecture of their homes might change from decade to decade, but the people remain eternally the same, forever themselves.

At the center of the stories is Archie himself, a wholesome if goofy and girl-crazy teenager, for whom the mundane world is rife with dangers. For Archie, as for teens everywhere and at all times, the common objects of daily existence are apt to take on a life of their own, and the mysterious ire of adults seems as easily provoked by his well-intentioned attempts to please as by his high jinks. When it comes to girls, Archie is hopelessly confused. His only stable relationship is with his jalopy. In short, Archie is the embodiment of adolescent awkwardness.

Forsythe P. "Jughead" Jones, Archie's pal, is no less awkward in his own way, but he is less, so to speak, involved. Essentially asocial, Jughead hates girls and loves hamburgers—indeed, food of all kinds, none of which ever seems to affect his weight. A loner, Jughead has often been considered the most complicated of the Archie crew, the weird sidekick of the popular average Joe. The basic model for Jughead had been around in popular American literature since Huck Finn first hung out with Tom Sawyer, but one suspects the character owes a lot to original artist Bob Montana, himself an outsider and a loner in high school. It is as if he gave Jughead his personality, just as he gave Archie his looks. It is Jughead's aloofness from the emotions driving the other major teenage characters, his very weirdness, that gives him perspective on the shenanigans taking place in Riverdale. Of course, Jughead's asocial habits often make him seem the sanest of the entire gang.

The gleefully self-centered Veronica Lodge, America's premier high school rich girl, is a middle-American fantasy. Implied in her interest in Archie is at least a questioning of the ease and leisure provided by Mr. Lodge. Her money did not seem to have made her a snob, which for the average reader would be unforgivable, but it did produce a charming teaser, whose manipulations, appearing so natural, seem all but harmless in the long run. If her rivalry with Betty is an indulgence, it is a consuming one, making the wealthy subdeb appear to be one of us, after all.

In many ways, Betty Cooper—America's quintessential Girl

TOP: *From "Double Date,"* **Archie #7** *(March–April 1944);* BOTTOM: *from* **Pep #31** *(September 1942)*

OPPOSITE, TOP TO BOTTOM: *From "Sugar Substitute,"* **Archie and Me #47** *(February 1972); cover of* **Archie's Christmas Love-in,** *January 1980; from* **Jughead #1** *(1949), featuring Jughead's little cousin, Souphead.*

Next Door—is defined by Veronica's jealousy as much as she is by her feelings for Archie. For it is their rivalry that elevates her schoolgirl crush to the level of myth. Betty's attraction to Archie is more visceral than Veronica's, and her methods for "catching" him—as she would be the first to admit—are more direct, more physical, more honest. Betty is a down-to-earth girl, with a vulnerable and sensitive side that occasionally breaks through the boy-crazy facade. If Archie's male readers understand his attraction to Veronica, its female readers understand Betty's attraction to him—and that makes the triangular formula work.

Reggie Mantle may actually be a more typical teenage American male than Archie, though fewer of us want to see ourselves in Reggie than we do in Archie or even Jughead. Sure, he is rich, but more importantly he is a confident and devious braggart, always looking out for himself, always trying to turn every situation to his own advantage. Seen from the outside, most high school boys are like that. Seen from the inside, only their rivals are. Hence, the handsome, self-assured, impeccably dressed Reggie, immediately recognizable as an American type, makes the perfect nemesis for the Archie we all imagined ourselves to be.

These five characters form the adolescent nucleus of the *Archie* stories. Around them orbit a number of adult foils. There is Mr. Lodge, Veronica's rich father, who always dresses like a pre-war diplomat and who loves Veronica with the same kind of blind devotion that Archie lavishes on his jalopy. With the aid of his snobbish and trusted butler, Smithers, he has spent a lifetime trying to have Archie removed from the premises. Fred Andrews, Archie's father, time and again proves that Archie's goofiness is in part hereditary, while his wholesome wife, Mary, is the sensible mother all Americans have come to expect from popular entertainment.

If Archie's parents are permanently perturbed, Pop Tate never is. Owner of the Chocklit Shoppe, the rotund Pop understands the kids like no other adult, perhaps because he sees more of them.

And more: The bumbling blowhard Mr. Weatherbee, Riverdale High's principal; Miss Grundy, the archetypal crone of a teacher; Coach Kleats, who seems to teach every varsity sport at Riverdale; Mr. Flutesnoot, the high school science teacher who boldly goes where no man has gone before each time he lets Archie mix chemicals in the lab; Miss Beazly, the cafeteria worker who brazenly serves the worst cuisine in America: high-school cafeteria food; the endearing Mr. Svenson, the school's Swedish janitor—all these make up the strange universe that passes for public education in Archie comics.

The five main Archie characters have their supporting cast, each with his or her personality "tags": Moose McGee (later to be renamed Moose Mason), big, dumb, and preternaturally jealous; Midge Clump, his sweet, passive girlfriend; Big Ethel Muggs, who after her fashion has as strong a crush on Jughead as Betty has on Archie, and whose approach to romance is even more direct; Dilton Doiley, the short, bespectacled brain of the school; Jughead's wiseacre little cousin, Souphead; there is even Jughead's overgrown pet, Hot Dog. These characters were joined in the seventies by some ethnic classmates: Chuck Clayton, a new black student, and the Hispanic Frankie Valdez, with their respective girlfriends Nancy and Maria. Chuck's father works for Coach Kleats as assistant varsity coach.

The trick is that everybody is familiar, and nothing ever changes. In a daring move, the company tried in the eighties to develop Jughead's character a bit by having him not only discover girls, but, like Archie, find himself torn between two adolescent beauties. The fans, from age seven to fifteen, revolted. They wanted the "old" Jughead—wacky, somnolent, enigmatic—back, avoiding the amorous advances of Big Ethel, prone to sleeping his life away, loving food, and hating girls. Suddenly, Jughead was jilted and returned to his former ways, announcing forthrightly, in a poem called "What I Think," that girls—all girls—"stink!"

If changing the characters is off limits, exploring their pasts is not, as the 1956 creation of Little Archie proved. Bob Bolling, the artist who produced the Little Archie stories, explored new plots and characters by concentrating on the adventures of the gang in elementary school. Consistently excellent, written and drawn with great sensitivity, Bolling's tales often struck at the heart. Believable characters with real emotions and clever story lines led Bolling to many a poignant moment and often a moral lesson.

Still, it was the teenage Archie who played center stage in a proliferating number of titles. And it was the teenage Archie—the eternal adolescent—whose goofy, girl-crazy personality inspired any number of imitations, from Dobie Gillis to Richie Cunningham.

The Past Without Pain

Comic books owed their existence to the turmoil of the late thirties, when the Depression destroyed homes and uprooted families, gangsters became an American institution, secretly admired though publicly admonished, and Hitler seemed not just a personification of evil, but terrifyingly successful in his bid for unlimited power. The old faiths and traditional values lost their hold on many Americans. Superman, strange visitor from another planet, completely good, incredibly strong, extremely patriotic, is vintage thirties wish fulfillment, straight and simple—a modern fantasy about old virtues.

Just as the late thirties cried out for a Superman, the coming of World War II helped create the longing for an Archie. As the management of MLJ Comics realized, *Archie*'s initial surge of popularity came from soldiers overseas, who saw in the escapades of the youngsters from Riverdale a gloss on the innocent lives they believed they had left behind but also were fighting to preserve. For them, mired in the horrors of world war, the reassuring normality of *Archie*'s world was its principal attraction.

But *Archie*'s popularity outlasted the war, just as *Superman* outlasted the late thirties. As Brian Walker of the Museum of Cartoon Art said recently in the *Boston Globe*: "Archie is one of the classic icons . . . the *Archie* strip is a blueprint for every modern-day teen sitcom from 'Dobie Gillis' to 'Happy Days.'" The wish fulfillment behind *Superman,* the daydream of unlimited power, is more basic than the historic circumstances that gave birth to it. And so is the appeal of Riverdale.

One secret of *Archie*'s appeal was as old as comics themselves: slapstick humor. For Bob Montana, with his early roots in vaudeville, slapstick must have seemed second nature. From the beginning, his Archie Andrews managed to create an air of anarchy about him. In his first appearance, showing off for a pubescent Betty Cooper, who has just moved into the neighborhood, Archie smashes his head through a cherished portrait of Betty's father, clips one of the burly movers in the chin with the end of a rake, rips a hole in his best pair of pants, and splatters Mr. Cooper with a vat of taffy. In his very next appearance, he wreaks havoc on the entire town by freeing a group of hounds from the dogcatcher's

OPPOSITE AND BELOW: From Pep *#22 (December 1941); TOP: from* Jackpot *#4, winter 1941; BOTTOM: from "Camera Bugs,"* Pep *#48 (May 1944)*

wagon in order to use them in the class play, *Uncle Tom's Cabin*.

It was a kind of humor thoroughly familiar to the devoted readers of the funny papers. For decades, characters like Happy Hooligan had been bungling their way into one catastrophe after another and winding up in jail for things they'd never done. The Katzenjammer Kids' delight in petty mischief, which each week threatened to lead to chaos yet always merely resulted in another spanking, had kept *two* strips—and several imitations—alive for half a century.

Archie Andrews, however, was a much more "realistic" character than Hans and Fritz Katzenjammer, those graphic ciphers of a childhood impulse, or Happy Hooligan, who did not even look human. The adults in Archie's world had reasons for being there. They were parents, or principals, or schoolteachers, even the owner of the local soda shop, instead of the exotic icons of adult authority—Mama, and the Cap'n (not a father, not a boarder, what?), or the ubiquitous Hooligan cops (just as stupid and one-dimensional as Gloomy Gus or Hooligan himself)—that peopled the dailies. The anarchy in Archie's personality was masked behind the natural awkwardness of the teenage years, and the slapstick humor was stripped of its ethnic slurs and its overt cruelty. Archie never wound up in jail, never received the ritualistic paddling; he lived in the suburbs and, at worst, was kept after school.

An even greater appeal of the original

Archie stories was their repressed sensuality. "*Archie* was pretty sexy stuff," says Brian Walker, "the way Bob Montana drew it." And, indeed, it is hard not to agree with him. Betty Cooper's coy stance in the splash panel of the first *Archie* story; Veronica Lodge undressing in the back of a limousine on the way to pick up her father in *Pep #31;* the shapely legs Archie photographs as an unknown woman in an alley lifts her skirt in the classic "Camera Bugs"; Veronica taking a shower in the daily paper on February 18, 1946; these and myriad other images led a generation of boys to romantic longings for Betty and (even more) Veronica—for the most part, secret longings.

Once again, the suggestive poses and asides of some of the early *Archie* stories were nothing new to regular readers of the comics. In 1912 *Polly and Her Pals* debuted, and by the 1920s a number of comely urban bachelor girls had appeared in the dailies, including *Fritzi Ritzi* (a strip that later came to center on Fritzi's niece Nancy) and even *Blondie.* Harold Foster's *Tarzan* first appeared on January 7, 1929, and was followed in the thirties by a group of exotic adventure strips—Alex Raymond's *Flash Gordon,* Lyman Young's *Tim Tyler's Luck,* Frank Miller's *Barney Baxter,* Roy Crane's *Captain Easy,* and Milton Caniff's *Terry and the Pirates*—that specialized in the en-

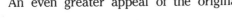

ticingly realistic portrayal of sexily clad women.

Those women, for all their illustrative realism, were exotic creatures far removed from everyday life, whereas *Archie*'s girls were neither so realistically rendered nor so unimaginably unobtainable. The effect was curious. You knew the Dragon Lady would do whatever you wanted or could imagine, but you would never meet her. On the other hand, you probably had already met a Betty or a Veronica, but you knew neither of them was "that kind of girl." They lived in the suburbs, after all.

Al Capp achieved something similar in *Li'l Abner* a few years earlier. There was no more suggestively drawn woman in all of comic history than Daisy Mae (except, perhaps, for Capp's own Passionata von Climax), yet somehow Daisy Mae's sexuality was rendered harmless by the fact that she came from Dog Patch, where the bombshells were too naive and the hunks too stupid to know with what they were bursting.

The comparison is especially interesting if we believe Capp's story about originally showing his idea for the strip to John Connolly, president of the King Features Syndicate, in 1934. Connolly's response was: "Great strip, great art; yes, sir. A couple of things, though— that Abner's an idiot. Make him a nice kid, with some saddlestripe shoes on him. And Daisy Mae's pretty; but how about some pretty clothes? As a matter of fact, why don't you forget that mountain bit and move them all to New Jersey?"

Or to Riverdale; what Capp made explicit, Montana simply implied. And he did it by creating a Riverdale so absolutely ordinary that it quite belied the obvious sensuality of the central relationships. It's there, beneath the surface, never mentioned, always present, *just like in high school*. It was Riverdale's wonderful normality that allowed *Archie* from the start to capture, in Brian Walker's words, "many adolescents' sexual awakening within the conser-

vative confines of a comic book."

It was not only the ambiguity of the relationships, but also their unchanging quality that helped to capture the reality of adolescence. For every adolescent knows he does not have the ability to change his life. Even as we experience them, the teen years seem eternal, partly because—since school is a given— social life feels institutional, *jail-like*, and partly because the explosion of hormones makes each moment of teenage life seem as if it will go on forever. What better place to catch that feeling but in a comic, where things are always the same; where, *just like in high school*, you have no real say over who your acquaintances—or even your friends—are? This feeling is captured quite well in the hockey story from *Archie #1,* where Jughead finds Archie haunting even his nightmares. In the long run, too, the "fixing" of the *Archie* stories firmly within the teen years would lead to the functioning of the adolescent characters as a middle-class "gang," a more wholesome version of the Dead End Kids of a generation before.

Finally, of course, there was the appeal of Riverdale itself. In the early stories, Riverdale's location does not seem much of a mystery. When Veronica first arrives at Riverdale High, she is a "subdeb" who has just moved into town (or just dropped down for the weekend, depending on which of the three versions of her arrival one follows) from Boston. And when Mr. Lodge makes his first definitive appearance a few months later, Riverdale is clearly located in

In this early Montana story from Archie #1 *(winter 1942), the artist develops Jughead's character against that of Archie. For many readers, Jughead is the most complex of the* Archie *characters.*

Massachusetts. From this it is only natural to assume that Riverdale is a suburban town not too distant from Boston, much like the Haverhill where Montana went to high school.

Fairly quickly in the development of *Archie,* however, geographical references disappeared, and Riverdale became one of the comics' mythological spaces, taking its place in a long line that stretched from the Yellow Kid's Hogan's Alley, through Skeezit's Gasoline Alley, and Superman's Metropolis (or Smallville) to Batman's Gotham City. But Riverdale had neither the ethnic flavor of Hogan's Alley, nor the neighborhood ambience of Gasoline Alley; it was devoid of Smallville's charm and Gotham City's brooding shadows; it was deliberately characterless, like the suburbs to which its readers would move.

The standardization of American life—and, with it, the American townscape—that had been going on since the First World War came close to being complete by the end of the Second. People yearned for a return to normality, and that yearning was reflected in where they lived and how they acted. *Archie's* Riverdale, with its lack of distinguishing features, perfectly anticipated the postwar trend toward the embrace of the ordinary. To *Archie's* readers, Riverdale looks like no place in particular; that is, like where they imagine they grew up or wished they were growing up.

And that is precisely why Riverdale and *Archie* proved so popular with the soldiers abroad, now returning home after the war. Like many fictional places abstracted from real life—Winesburg, Ohio, or Yaknapataphwa County, Mississippi, for example—Riverdale grew from a nostalgic impulse. *Nostalgia,* a word coined by an Alsatian medical student named Johannes Hofer from Greek roots meaning "home" and "pain," was for centuries considered an actual disease. Fed by Romantic-era literature and a rapid industrialization that was destroying all sense of place, nostalgia, by the middle of the nineteenth century, came to

mean not mere "homesickness," but the sense of loss of one's personal past and of the historical past as well. By the mid-twentieth century, nostalgia was ubiquitous, and Americans, set down between an ominous future and a vanished, idealized past, clung to the things, the objects, the memories that aroused in them associations of purity and simplicity, of an authenticity they thought they'd lost. A good many of them, some million plus, were nostalgic for the world as it existed in *Archie,* a world they had never really known.

For young Americans in the forties, Riverdale *was,* at least emotionally, their high school hometown. Wartime nostalgia had allowed Montana and the others at MLJ to combine the internal anarchy of childhood with the incipient sensuality of adolescence into a simple and emotionally satisfying portrait of an idealized past we can all share. Archie's proneness to trouble and his girl-crazy nature, Jughead's hatred and fear of women, Betty's heedless infatuation, Veronica's manipulative coyness, Reggie's braggadocio call to mind the jubilant turmoil of youth sans its doubts and anguish. After being on the edge of destruction, that was all *Archie's* first readers wanted: the past (and the future) back, without pain.

It is what we all want still.

In comic art, realism had always been the exclusive province of the exotic or glamorous daily strips and the action-oriented comic books. The "homey" strips, the comics concentrating on everyday life and common things, had for some reason always relied on stylization and caricature. Now, with the public looking for straight strips about conventional people "realistically" portrayed, the two techniques drew closer together. MLJ, by combining the two strains of sequential art, had created a salable formula that would survive a postwar Establishment attack on comic books in general, the advent of television, and an apparently substantial change in the nature—and age—of comic-book readership.

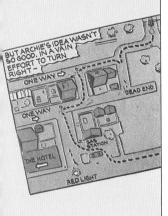

From Pep #25 *(March 1942)*

The final ingredient of the Archie *formula* was added in Archie #7 (March–April 1944), in a story called "Double Date." The first definitive love story established clearly and unambiguously the eternal triangle between Archie, Betty, and Veronica, pitting the two girls against one another in competition for the boy. Unique to the Archie comics, this three-way relationship is key to their continuing popularity.

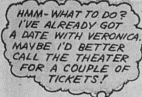

NOW TO GO GET BETTY. **WHAT A SPOT!** I GOTTA BE IN TWO PLACES AT TH' SAME TIME TONIGHT!

C'MON, BETTY, LET'S MAKE WITH THE SPEED!

GOSH, ARCHIE, I THOUGHT YOU WERE NEVER COMING BACK!

ER...AH... YOU SURE YOU WOULDN'T RATHER GO TOMORROW NIGHT, BETTY?

OF COURSE I'M SURE! WHAT IN TH' WORLD'S COME OVER YOU, ARCHIE! YOU'RE NERVOUS AS A CAT!

WHERE ARE THESE SEATS LOCATED BUD! NOT IN THE ORCHESTRA, I HOPE!

BROTHER, YOU SURE GOT YOUR HOPE! UPSTAIRS!

YEAH— I KNOW UP!

UP!

UP!

BUT ARCHIE! WHERE ARE YOU GOING?

SIT DOWN!

QUIET!

JUST SIT DOWN AND ENJOY THE SHOW, BETTY..I..UH .. HAVE A HEADACHE **AND WHAT A HEADACHE!** BE RIGHT BACK!

TSK, TSK

In Archie #1, *Montana chose to revise the story of Veronica Lodge's debut in Riverdale. In the story, "Prom Pranks," Veronica has grown sexier and more manipulative—the classic teenage American subdeb.*

HERE WE HAVE ONE OF THOSE TYPICAL *QUIZ KIDS*, SOLVING A TERRIFIC ADVANCED TRIGONOMETRY PROBLEM -- AT LEAST THAT'S WHAT THE TEACHER THOUGHT IT WAS! SHE WASN'T SURE!

BUT WHAT ABOUT ONE OF THE QUIZ KIDS IN THE NEXT ROOM? WHAT MOMENTOUS PROBLEM IS TAXING *HIS* BRAIN?

LET ME SEE -- HOW DO YOU SPELL SUPER-DUPER?

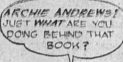

ARCHIE ANDREWS! JUST *WHAT* ARE YOU DOING BEHIND THAT BOOK?

WHO, ME? --- WHY, I'M -- EK -- WRITING AN *ESSAY*, MISS GRUNDY!

HMMMM! ARE YOU *SURE* THAT'S WHAT YOU'RE DOING?

OH, YES! --- I'M WRITING AN ESSAY ON SHAKESPEARE, HEH, HEH! AND I'M GOING TO MAKE IT THE *BEST* ESSAY I EVER WROTE FOR YOU!

PSSST! ARCHIE, YOU DOPE! THIS IS THE *GEOMETRY* CLASS!

MUCH LATER ---

GOSH! I THOUGHT SHE WAS GOING TO KEEP ME AFTER SCHOOL UNTIL TOMORROW MORNING!...HEY, THERE'S JUGHEAD! *HEY, JUGHEAD* ...WAIT!

GEE, JUGHEAD, I HOPE MISS GRUNDY DOESN'T FIND THAT LETTER! I THREW IT ON THE FLOOR BEHIND ME!

OH -- YOU DON'T HAVE TO WORRY ABOUT THAT, ARCHIE! *I* PICKED IT UP!

PAGE 6.

OH, YOU DID, HUH? AND I SUPPOSE YOU READ IT!

NOT A WORD! SAY, WHAT DID YOU WANT TO INVITE A SUB-DEB LIKE HER TO THE PROM FOR? WHEN DID YOU MEET HER?------- ---TWO ALL BLACKS, MAC!

♪♫...♪ ---FROM THE ...HALLS OF MONTEZ

SHUCKS! I *NEVER* MET HER! I WRITE LETTERS TO HER ALL THE TIME --- BUT I ALWAYS TEAR 'EM UP! I CAN ALWAYS DREAM, CAN'T I? SAY, WHAT DID YOU DO WITH MY LETTER YOU FOUND?

I MAILED IT!

PFFFFT!

TAKE IT EASY, DON JUAN! YOU KNOW THESE SOCIETY DAMES HAVE SECRETARIES! IT'LL PROBABLY END UP IN THE ASH CAN BEFORE VERONICA EVEN SEES IT!

JUST THE SAME, IT WAS A DUMB THING TO DO! WHY, IF ANYBODY EVER FOUND OUT----

THEN ARCHIE PICKED UP HIS "STEADY," *BETTY COOPER*...

ARCHIE, WHERE'S JUGHEAD?

OH, HE'S WALKING AHEAD! I WOULDN'T GIVE THAT GUY A RIDE ANYWAY!

AH----BETTY--- ---I WAS THINKIN' ER-- ABOUT THE PROM FRIDAY NIGHT---WOULD YOU LIKE TO GO WITH ME?

TO THE PROM? OH, ARCHIE, YOU DARLING!

HEY... ---MMMPH!

SMACK!

GOSH! I DIDN'T THINK ARCHIE WAS *THAT* SORE!

3.

PAGE 8

PAGE 10

THE STAG LINE...

G-GOSH! ISN'T SHE *GORGEOUS!*

YOU CAN SAY *THAT* AGAIN, BROTHER!

ARCHIE'LL GIVE US A *BREAK!* GO AHEAD, STREAKY, CUT IN!

YES, BUT REMEMBER THE RIVERDALE CODE, FELLAS!

THAT'S RIGHT DUSTY, WE GOTTA WAIT FOR ARCHIE'S OKAY!

PSSST! ARCHIE -- BETTY'S GETTING SORE AND MY FEET ARE KILLING ME!

OKAY! OKAY! I'LL BE RIGHT THERE!

LISTEN, MEN, WILL YA DO ME A FAVOR? KEEP VERONICA BUSY FOR A WHILE --- WILL YOU?

WILL WE

AND THE *MATRONS...* MR. WEATHERBEE! JUST LOOK AT THAT GIRL FROM NEW YORK ARCHIE ANDREWS BROUGHT!

THAT GOWN! IT'S SHOCKING! YOU MUST DO SOMETHING!

HARRUMPH! ALL RIGHT! I'LL SPEAK TO HER!

HEY! GET IN LINE --- OOPS!! SORRY, MR. WEATHERBEE!

AHEM! YOUNG LADY!

WHY, YOU'RE MR. WEATHERBEE, THE PRINCIPAL! AREN'T YOU SWEET TO WANT TO DANCE WITH ME!

*"Camera Bugs,"
from* Pep #48
*(May 1948), is a
good example of
the best stories
from* Archie's *first
decade—leisurely
paced by current
comic-book stan-
dards and playful
in both story line
and graphic
action. The
theme—the aver-
age American's
mismatch with
technology—
would become a
favorite not just
of future* Archie
*stories, but of
popular entertain-
ment in general.*

55

HELLO, YES! THIS IS WEATHERBEE!

WELL! YOU CERTAINLY TAKING THIS MATTER VERY LIGHTLY! WE'RE HAVING A SPECIAL MEETING ABOUT YOU RIGHT NOW!

GULP! WHAT'D I DO NOW?

GULP!

MAYBE THEY FOUND OUT ABOUT THAT TICKET I BOUGHT FOR THE RAFFLE!

WEATHERBEE PRINCIPAL

WHERE IS HE? WHERE'S THAT OLD LOTHARIO?

YOU...YOU OLD REPRO BATE! I'M TAKING MY DAUGHTER OUT OF THIS SCHOOL AT ONCE!

BUT, BUT! PLEASE... WHAT'D I DO?

AS IF YOU DIDN'T KNOW! LOOK AT THIS!!

OWN & GOLD

AWK

BROWN & GOLD

RIVERDALE HIGH'S OWN PAPER
WEATHERBEE.. MAN OF ACTION!!?

LATER-- .. THEN, HE SAYS, TAKE THAT BLANKETY-BLANK CAMERA!

YEAH,.. I KNOW.. RELAX WILL YA?

TIRED & LISTLESS, LAZY? TSK-TSK!

POP, I DON'T WISH TO SEEM UNGRATEFUL, BUT I DON'T THINK I'LL USE THIS CAMERA ANYMORE!

NONSENSE, M'BOY! DON'T GET DISCOURAGED!

I'LL SHOW YOU HOW TO TAKE PICTURES! THERE'S NOTHING TO IT!

YEAH! THAT'S WHAT GRUNDY SAID!

SEE NOW-- JUST TAKE A SIMPLE SUBJECT LIKE THAT..

IT'S SIMPLE NOW, ANYWAY!

SEE, ARCH, IT'S AS SIMPLE AS "A" "B" "C"!

CLICK

ONE HOUR LATER

Archie aficionados consider "No Body's Dummy," from Pep #64 (November 1947), possibly the funniest story to appear during the 1940s. The high jinks and hysteria, a legacy of the newspaper funnies, are here given ample room to develop into an almost self-generating narrative, like many of the "Three Stooges" episodes. Those familiar only with the post-Comics Code Authority stories may be surprised by both the broadness of the humor and its slapstick violence.

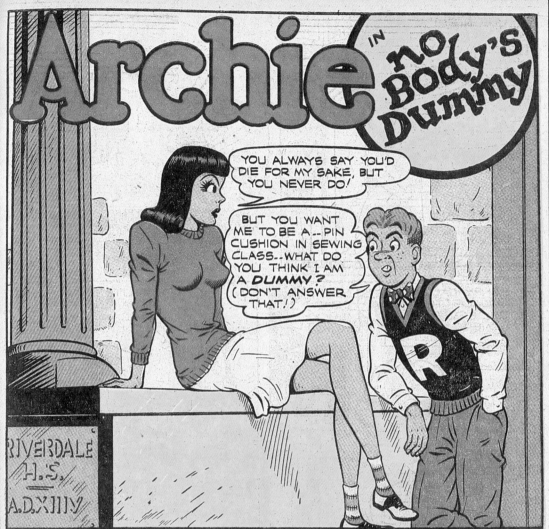

YIPE! NOW WHO PUT A BOTTLE OF RED INK UP THERE?

GET READY.. HE'S MAKING A GETAWAY!

CAN I SHOOT, CHIEF?

DAD RAT IT! I'LL HAVE TO WASH THIS RED INK OFF!

KONK!

DARN THESE SYNTHETIC RUBBER GARTERS.. BROKE AGAIN! HMMM... NO ONE IN THE OFFICE!

AH, WETHERBEE ISN'T HERE! I CAN GET MY DUMMY BACK!

I'LL DUCK BEHIND THIS CLOSET DOOR AND USE A PAPER CLIP!

WELL, PUT THE DUMMY BEHIND THAT SCREEN AND I'LL GET IT WHEN WE ARE READY!

I'LL STOP IN THIS EMPTY ROOM AND STRAIGHTEN MY WIG!

EEEK!

RIGHT IN SCHOOL... KISSING AND HUGGING... WELL! I NEVER!

SHE'S RIGHT... SHE NEVER!

HA! I KNEW IT! ARCHIE!... AND I'LL BET THE HUSSY IS VERONICA!

CLOCKWISE: Archie #1 (winter 1942); Archie #27 (July–August 1947); Archie #28 (September–October 1947); Archie #30 (January–February 1948); Laugh #32 (April 1949)

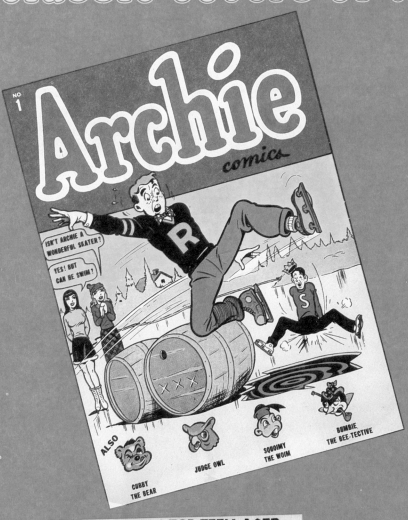

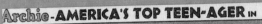

T he characters, stories, and settings in the Archie comics so perfectly captured the country's vision of what it means to be a teenager that they took on a life of their own, beyond the pages of the comics themselves. The images produced by Archie's artists and writers became both the icons of youth in American popular culture and the foundation for a business empire.

In the forties, a radio show called "The Adventures of Archie Andrews" was the first big boost to the multimedia career of Riverdale's favorite son. Starring Jackie Grimes as Archie and Arnold Stang as Jughead, the show was broadcast Monday through Friday over the now defunct Blue Network. With the advent of television and the tradition of Saturday-morning cartoons, Archie starred over the years in a number of network and syndicated TV cartoon shows. Along with a number of other characters generated by Archie Enterprises, but not part of the Archie family (Sabrina, the Teen-Age Witch; Josie and the Pussycats), Archie had by the late sixties become standard Saturday-morning fare, with the most popular of the Archie shows hitting a record-breaking 75 percent Nielsen audience share on CBS.

One of those nationally syndicated cartoon shows centered around a rock'n' roll band called The Archies, which consisted of Archie on guitar, Reggie on bass, Jughead on drums, Veronica on organ, and Betty on tambourine. Actually, the band was a group of studio musicians, with Ron Dante as lead singer, who had a string of hits with CBS Records in the early seventies, including "Jingle, Jangle," "Bang Shang-a-Lang," and one of the top-selling singles of the decade, "Sugar, Sugar."

Archie has appeared on prime-time television in live-action shows twice. The first time, on December 19, 1976, David Caruso played the red-headed teenager. Most recently, on May 6, 1990, Christopher Rich starred as an adult Archie attending a high-school reunion in NBC's "To Riverdale and Back Again." At this writing, a major motion picture featuring Archie's pals and gals is in the works.

In the seventies, Archie became a public company, Archie Enterprises, Inc., and the licensing of the trademark characters proliferated. There were Archie games, Archie puzzles, Archie coloring books, Archie lunch boxes, Archie wristwatches, Archie toys. Archie's jalopy, Lizzie, became an automobile model. The faces of Archie, Jughead, Veronica, Betty, Reggie, Big Moose, Mr.

Weatherbee, Miss Grundy, and others appeared on T-shirts and jars of Welch's jam and jelly. In the Midwest, a string of Archie restaurants opened.

But the cornerstone of the business remained publishing. The number of individual titles, from the venerable Pep to the latest Riverdale High, would vary, reaching a high in the seventies of thirty-four. At one point, Montana's daily and Sunday syndicated strip was carried by more than six hundred newspapers. Archie has published a series of educational comics to help motivate students and teach them to read. For the last two decades, the company has produced a series of religious comic books using the Archie characters to spread the New Testament gospel. These comic books were distributed, under license, to religious bookstores by Spire Christian Comics and are presently distributed by Barbour Christian Comics. Finally, in addition to its regular comic-book titles, Archie also issues 5-by-7-inch digest magazines of comic stories, puzzles, and gags.

Archie and his friends have become the emotional (if not legal) property of an entire culture. There have been Archie look-alike contests (some sponsored by the company) and Archie dances. Mad magazine ran a classic parody of the gang called "Starchie," which as much as anything indicates how official a figure Archie has become. (And not just Archie; in February 1980, Jughead appeared on the cover of Atlantic Monthly to announce that the S.A.T. tests were "culturally biased.") In fact, Archie seems almost naturally to come to the minds of newspaper reporters, magazine writers, and book authors when they write about the young. The carrot-topped culture hero is often invoked, and his image is often used as a touchstone of the "average" American teen.

A real-life Archie, Betty, Veronica, and Jughead? These are winners of the Archie look-alike contest.

Early on, Archie characters were incarnated as dolls and play figures as well as featured on lunch boxes, glasses, mugs, even wristwatches. By 1991, Archie, Inc., had forty-two American and Canadian product licenses.

A Formula for Success

Most comics, like most popular entertainment everywhere, tend toward the ritual repetition of generic formulas. Whether comic images spring from the realms of fantasy, or out of wish fulfillment, or from projections of power, sooner or later we learn to recognize as typical the concrete-and-steel canyons of Superman's Metropolis, the dark alleys of Batman's Gotham City, or the standardized suburbia of Archie's Riverdale High and to expect that we will see there certain characters we know well, acting in situations for the most part familiar. The repetitiveness is part of the pleasure; the comfort it brings is the key to the success of almost all serial fiction.

Once that formula is in place, it seems to operate on its own. Innumerable artists have drawn a Superman, a Batman, or an Archie with varying degrees of success, but with hardly any damage to the long-term popularity of the formula itself. Even moribund fictional characters like Sir Arthur Conan Doyle's Sherlock Holmes, Edgar Rice Burroughs's Tarzan, or Ian Fleming's James Bond have been successfully revived, and a number of artists have carried on daily strips after the original creator was fired, quit, or died.

Most successful generic formulas, however, do not pop into existence full blown. They take time to develop. And in 1941 and 1942, that is precisely what Bob Montana was doing with the *Archie* stories—developing a successful new series formula.

The Archie who made his quiet, if historic, debut in December 1941 was, like the Betty and Jughead who accompanied him, barely a teenager. He hated his name, instructed Betty to call him "Chick," and acted much as Tom Sawyer might have acted if he'd been born in the twentieth rather than the nineteenth century. Jughead, Archie's Huck Finn, was more ragamuffin than he would ever be again, wearing patched pants along with his omnipresent hat. Riverdale, too, seemed more Twainesque and small-town instead of suburban, with its Saturday Carnival, "the biggest event in Riverdale history."

By winter 1942, *Archie* was being billed as "The Mirth of a Nation," and the young man was wearing an early version of his trademark letter sweater. Clearly

older, perhaps the seventeen-going-on-eighteen he would remain for the next fifty years, Archie was soon endowed by Montana with a car—the jalopy, one day to be named "Lizzie," that he loved before all else, and whose wheels, when in motion, never touched the ground. A high school principal arrived on the scene simultaneously with the automobile, but though he was balding, he was far thinner than the soon-to-be-famous Mr. Weatherbee.

In fact, it took several issues of *Pep* and *Jackpot* for the artist to settle on the appropriate adult foil. The plump, toupee-topped, easily rattled Weatherbee did not make his debut till spring 1942, in *Jackpot #5*. In that same story, a loudmouthed classmate named Reggie Mantle makes his debut, but readers would have to wait yet one more issue to get a full introduction to Archie's rich-boy rival. Along with Weatherbee, there also appeared a stern and aged teacher, then called Miss Scott.

As Weatherbee had, she too would evolve. In one of the earliest Archie stories, Montana had introduced in a single panel a strangely behatted hag called Mrs. (later, "Miss") Grundy as the Riverdale principal. She did not appear again until August 1942, when—in *Pep #30*—Montana revived the elderly schoolmarm, combined her with the earlier principal, and unleashed on the world the ultimate Miss Grundy, who sometimes taught science and sometimes history—but who could tell the difference?

By then, the Boston debutante Veronica Lodge had long ago arrived in town. It was on a morning in April 1942, a month after Archie got his wheels, that she walked into his life, and *Archie* would never be the same. "Egypt had its Cleopatra!" Montana wrote. "Hollywood its Hedy Lamarr!—And now Riverdale has its Veronica Lodge." Archie, of course, makes an immediate fool of himself, fighting for a ruler she has dropped—and he's been making a fool of himself over her for half a century.

She was, even for those of us who did not

see her that first day as she walked into Riverdale High, worth it. Rich and beautiful, shapely and refined, cool and manipulative, is she not every American male's dream of the woman he wants to marry? And wants to, even knowing that if he does, he'll live to regret it; wants to, even believing—as *she* does—that she is better than he; wants to, even understanding he can never be much more than a convenient escort.

In that first story, Veronica is almost too

nice. After Archie retrieves her dropped ruler, she accepts his invitation to dinner immediately, almost as if she might be charmed by the young man. In any case, there is lacking the clear notion that she is deigning to accept Archie's offering in order to reward properly obsequious male behavior—that sense of *calculation* mixed with basically naive rich-girl assumptions about the world that will in future be essential to her character.

In fact, she is totally unconscious of the trouble she causes Archie throughout the story. When he shows up for their date, she suggests that he take her to an expensive restaurant not *in spite of* the fact that she knows he has no money, but simply because she has heard (from her no doubt wealthy acquaintances) that the restaurant is a good one. That it happens to be the restaurant where Archie has been working in order to earn extra money for this very date is coincidental, a function of plot rather than Veronica's character.

When Archie seems to know the waiters, she is duly impressed. The manager, of course, spies Archie in the tuxedo he has borrowed from the restaurant for his date and puts him to work. To cover the fact that he is serving—as well as having—dinner, Archie introduces Veronica to other young men at the restaurant and invites her to dance with them. Veronica goes along with his peculiar behavior, exhibiting a patience few women—rich or poor, young or old—would. Only when she leaves with one of the other boys do we get a hint of the Veronica we will come to know. But even that happens offstage, while Archie is spending hours washing dishes in the back without telling her, and her behavior is perfectly understandable.

The conflict is all Archie's. It grows from a simple contrast between his penury and Veronica's social status. When Archie tells Betty at the end of the story that he wants nothing more to do with debutantes, it's because he can't afford them, not because Veronica has intentionally toyed with him in some way. Al-

most immediately, Montana would correct his mistake and create a Veronica clearly aware of the differences between herself and the other kids of Riverdale. From that change, the "classic" *Archie* stories spring, driven by the emotionally fixed relationships as much as by the situational comedy of the plots.

After a half-dozen appearances, Archie had become so popular that MLJ decided to give the kid his own book and commissioned Montana, already leaving for the Army, to create *Archie Comics #1*. Montana took the opportunity to revise the story of Veronica's opening night at Riverdale High.

This time, she lives in Boston, and Archie sees her debutante picture in the society pages. He writes her a love letter inviting her to the prom, which Jughead mails despite the fact that Arch has already asked Betty. Back in Boston, Veronica—clad only in a nightgown, while her mother nearby is fully dressed—reads Archie's letter and bursts into laughter, leaning languorously across her cushioned divan, stretching her shapely legs right out of the panel. She condescendingly decides to accept the invitation—as a joke. In the end, after catching poison ivy at the prom because of Archie, she remains in town a few days for treatment and, spoiled to the end, decides to stay and attend Riverdale High for a while in

ABOVE: From Pep *#26 (April 1942); LEFT: from* Archie *#1 (winter 1942)*

order to take up some "unfinished business" with one Archie Andrews.

Despite the improbable conclusion, the story does establish Veronica's character—spoiled, careless, condescending, aware of her social position and her wealth, though still often unconscious of her own motives—more effectively than when she first appeared. And it was the story Montana would stick with when he returned after the war to pen *Archie* as a syndicated newspaper strip, though he would modify Veronica's motivation for accepting the invitation and play more subtly with the psychology of mother and daughter. In time, Veronica's parents would follow her to Riverdale, and their butler, Smithers, and her father would make a vocation of tossing Archie out the front door of their mansion.

Readers had the pleasure of meeting Veronica's father a few months before *Archie #1* appeared. Variously known as Lancelot Lodge, Hiram Lodge, John P. Lodge, even *Dr.* Lodge, it was as Burton K. Lodge, Big Shot Massachusetts Politician, that he first flew down to Riverdale in September 1942 to see what his daughter was up to. Through a series of blunders, Archie both irrevocably angers Mr. Lodge and, as Veronica says in the closing panel, "Practically put him in the governor's chair."

So far as it goes, the story is the first of thousands of such encounters between the two. In and of itself, it is not all that remarkable. What *is* remarkable is Veronica's role.

As the story opens in *Pep #31,* Veronica is poised in a bathing suit on the edge of the high school pool, wiggling what *she* might call her derriere. She wins the meet, and as Archie congratulates her, she receives a telegram announcing her father's arrival. She asks Archie to drive her to the airport. On the way to the car, her robe blows back, revealing her bathing suit–clad, leggy body, and she insists on taking her car to the airport so she can change into her clothes in the back seat *en route.* As Archie gulps, a nearby man of the cloth, who has

overheard, covers his mouth in disapproval as his own eyes (perhaps) take a gander. Once inside, Veronica tells Archie not to peek, to keep his eyes on the road, and he gulps again. In the next panel we see a red-faced Archie, eyes fixed forward. From the back comes Veronica's voice: "How do you like driving my car, Archie?" He replies, they arrive at the airport, and a fully clad Veronica steps out, answering Archie's "Gee whiz, how did you do it?" with "Oh, a little trick I learned in an upper berth."

The ambiguity is delicious. Is she deliberately teasing? Is she simply in a hurry to see her father, typically preoccupied with herself and unconscious of the effect she's having on those around her? Montana is *certainly* teasing his audience with the entire situation, using the props of teenage seduction—the back seat of a car, rushing to get dressed before Daddy arrives—to underpin the doubt that is truly the source of Archie's awkwardness. We all know that doubt, and so what Archie is thinking is not ambiguous at all. Teenage life is rife with such moments.

For a number of reasons, including the establishment of the Comics Code Authority and the shift in *Archie*'s postwar readership to mostly preteens, no such scene could ever appear in *Archie* today. But scenes with the same kinds of ambiguity and playfulness were not uncommon in Montana's comic-book *Archie*.

Archie Comics #1 hit the stands in winter 1942, just about a year after Archie himself was

ABOVE: From "Like Real Gone," Laugh #104 *(November 1959);* RIGHT: *from* Pep #31 *(September 1942)*

born. The departing Montana provided in that premiere issue a one-page introduction to the principal characters called "Who's Who in Riverdale." There were Archie and his parents, Veronica, Betty, Jughead, Mr. Weatherbee, and Miss Grundy. Reggie, already introduced, was absent, however. And something else, too, was missing: Betty and Veronica's rivalry for Archie. The caption under Veronica points out that she thinks Archie is a "pushover—but hasn't decided which cliff." And Betty "can't make up her mind whether to go after the one that's handsome [Tyrone Power] and she'll *never* get, or the one she *can* get, that's Archie!" Though the rivalry between the two is nascent, perhaps, in the recap of Veronica's debut later in the issue, it had not yet become the focus of a single story and still did not define their relationship.

That rivalry would not come until *Archie #7,* March–April 1944, in a story titled, appropriately enough, "Double Date." Once again, Archie makes a date with both Veronica and Betty, just as he had long ago on prom night. After Archie and Betty win a pair of tickets to hear "the orchestra," she begs off and suggests he take Jughead with him. He invites Veronica instead, only to have Betty show up expecting to go when she discovers Jughead is staying home. Archie, being Archie, decides to take both girls, and borrows the money from Betty, "for an emergency," in order to purchase a second set of tickets. The story consists of his efforts to keep the two apart, only to have them catch him in the end and walk off together.

The main gimmick of the *Archie* formula was in place. From that point forward, Archie Comics writers and artists would focus on girls in competition for a boy instead of the age-old rivalry between males of the species for a female. And once again, the fixed nature of the formula would mirror the "eternal" relationships of adolescence. Hardly a teenage girl in America got through high school without experiencing such a rivalry with a friend, and because of the peculiar metabolic and social nature of the teen years, it seemed at the time that such tensions were endless.

Over the years, the rest of the *Archie* characters would develop: Coach Kleats, Riverdale High's gym teacher; Pop Tate, proprietor of Pop's Chocklit Shoppe; Big Moose and his well-protected girl, Midge; Dilton Doiley, Riverdale High's egghead; Big Ethel, the extraordinarily unattractive girl in love with Forsythe P. Jones, alias Jughead. And there was, of course, Reggie, Archie's chief rival for Veronica's affections. But, most often, the strip would highlight Betty and Veronica's battles over Archie, which have made him a permanent fixture of Americana.

TOP: *From* Archie *#1—in which Bob Montana used a full page to introduce the saga's main characters;* BOTTOM: *from "Double Date,"* Archie *#7 (March–April 1944)*

In the 1950s, the *Archie* stories began to focus more exclusively on the teenagers of Riverdale, their relationships, their worries, and their fads. The adults, who had figured prominently in many of the stories from the 1940s, faded somewhat into the background. And in stories such as "Like Real Gone," from Laugh #104 (November 1959), fads—here the style, language, and dress of the "beat generation"—provided the narrative drive of the story.

LIKE HI, DAD! WHAT'S BUGGIN' THE CHICKS?

SQUARESVILLE, MAN! **EIGHT** SIDED CUBES!--- THEY'RE NOT **OUT** HERE WITH US!

I GOT IT! I GOT IT!

OH, BETTY! N-NOT **YOU** TOO?

NO! NO, RON!

THESE JERKS! THEY'RE BEATNIKS!

YOU MEAN THOSE,-- THOSE **BUMS?**

OH, NO! NOT BUMS!

-BUMS, YOU CAN **UNDERSTAND!**

LIKE SCROOGEVILLE! A FEW BILLS OVER, AND HE CUTS OFF OUR SUPPLY!

LET'S CUT OVER TO YOUR CHICK'S PAD! SHE PACKS A FABULOUS FRIDGE!

LIKE CRAZY, MAN!

BONG! BONG!

HMPH! COME IN, IF YOU MUST!

HI, BIG DADDY!

YOUR CHICK IN THE PAD?

D-UH--- WHAT'D HE SAY? WHAT'D HE SAY?

DON'T MIND THEM, DADDY! THEY'RE BEATNIKS!

"BEATNIKS?"

LIKE WE'RE WITH IT, DAD!

OUT THERE! SPACEVILLE!

LET'S ROTATE THE CROPS, CHICK! COUSIN AND I ARE REAL LOW!

THE LOWEST!

ER-LIKE, THEY'RE FROM **HUNGER**?

YOU DIG IT, DADDY! **REAL** SHARP!

BIG DADDY, THAT'S A REAL FRANTIC KITTEN YOU'VE GOT!

THIS PAD IS THE MOST, MAN!

DIG THESE CRAZY ORANGE CRATES!

"ORANGE CRATES?" MY PRICELESS ANTIQUE FURNITURE?

PLAY IT COOL, DAD!

I'LL PLAY IT COOL!! I'D LIKE TO DEEP FREEZE THE TWO OF YOU!

TSK! HE BUGS EASY!

SMITHERS! THE BEAT GENERATION HAS INVADED MY HOUSE!

PREPARE TO REPEL BOARDERS!

MAN! DIG THAT FRANTIC SET OF THREADS!

THE COOLEST!

YOU CATS ARE FAR OUT!

THE FARTHEST, MAN!

(GROAN) I GUESS WE WEREN'T FAR ENOUGH OUT TO SUIT HIM!

SLAM!

WELL, SMITHERS? IS THE JOB DONE?

LIKE ENDSVILLE, DAD! YOUR PAD IS CLEAN! ANYTHING ELSE BUGGING YOU, LIKE RIGHT NOW, MAN?

LIKE SPREAD OUT, CATS!

LAMSVILLE!

THE END

In one of the best treatments of a "relevant" theme, "The Time of Your Life," from Betty and Veronica *#156 (December 1968), translates the mistrust born of the ill-named "generation gap" of the '60s into a funny story about the misperceptions born of prejudice and the blindness of authority.*

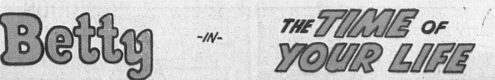

Betty -IN- THE TIME OF YOUR LIFE

DADDY, OUR CROWD IS GOING TO PICNIC AT THOSE LOVELY PUBLIC GARDENS ON ROUTE TWO! DO YOU KNOW IF THERE'S AN ADMISSION CHARGE?

I'M AFRAID I *DON'T*, BETTY!

BUT I HAVE TO PASS THAT WAY THIS MORNING! SUPPOSE I STOP IN AND ASK?

GREAT!

I HOPE THE ANSWER IS NEGATIVE! WE'RE NOT THE WEALTHIEST GROUP IN THE WORLD!

EVEN WITH VERONICA!

HAH! THAT'S WHAT THEY'D LIKE YOU TO THINK!

WE'VE HAD EXPERIENCE WITH TEENAGERS BEFORE, MISTER! WE KNOW WHAT TO EXPECT!

RIVERDALE PUBLIC PARK

NO ADMISSION? THAT'S GREAT!

ER... YOU DON'T HAVE ANYBODY NAMED *BONNIE*, OR *CLYDE* IN YOUR GROUP, DO YOU?

NO DADDY! WHY?

WELL, JUST DON'T EXPECT TOO WARM A GREETING AT THE GARDENS!

OH! THE TEENAGE SYNDROME AGAIN?

(SIGH) WE KNOW DADDY! JUSTICE AT WORK! I'M INNOCENT UNTIL PROVED GUILTY!

UNLESS YOU'RE A GROUP OF TEENAGERS!

③

Top row: Pep #116 *(July 1956);* Archie #95 *(September 1958);* Laugh #44 *(April 1951);*
Middle row: Laugh #43 *(February 1951);* Betty and Veronica #8 *(1952);* Laugh #45 *(June 1951);*
Bottom row: Betty and Veronica #112 *(April 1965);* Jughead #167 *(April 1969)*

Classic Covers of the 50s ...

& 60s

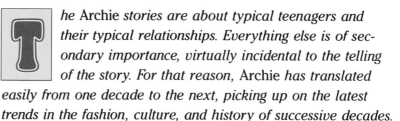

he Archie *stories are about typical teenagers and their typical relationships. Everything else is of secondary importance, virtually incidental to the telling of the story. For that reason,* Archie *has translated easily from one decade to the next, picking up on the latest trends in the fashion, culture, and history of successive decades.*

Archie's artists have made it a matter of pride to keep up with the latest in teen fashion, just as Archie's writers pay careful attention to teenage crazes for everything from the jitterbug to rap music. The fashion-conscious images grew to be an important part of Archie's appeal as the audience came increasingly to consist of preteen young women.

But beyond fashion, the different historical periods and their special concerns self-consciously shaped stories featuring the basically never-changing characters and situations. The times clearly announce themselves in 1945's "The Air Raid Warden" and 1948's "The Battle of the Jitterbugs." And those stories have their fifties counterparts in stories like "Skip, Hop, and Thump," centered around a sock hop, and "Like Real Gone," in which Archie and Jughead suddenly become beatniks. Occasionally, fashion itself is the subject of a strip, as in "New Look, Few Look," from 1956, or a current craze is parodied, as the rage for Elvis Presley in 1957's "Fan Clubbed."

The trendiness itself soon became a hallmark of Archie *comics. In the sixties, we get "The Man from R.I.V.E.R.D.A.L.E." (a takeoff on television's popular "The Man from U.N.C.L.E."). Following the success of the "Batman" TV series, Archie—who had singlehandedly banished superheroes from the MLJ Comics pantheon—becomes a superhero himself in "Pureheart the Powerful," which in time turned Jughead into Captain Hero, Betty into Superteen, and Reggie into Evilheart. When "Mary Hartman, Mary Hartman" had attracted a fanatical television audience, Betty began keeping a diary in stories called "Betty Cooper, Betty Cooper."*

In the early seventies, Jughead joined a commune in "Never Never Land," and Archie imitated the Fonz (whose "Happy Days" TV series owes much of its inspiration to Archie in the first place). The seventies, in general, saw the appearance of explicit social issues. "Weigh Out Scene" was touted in the New York Times *as a socially significant but subtle comment on racism and prejudice. In one 1970 issue, both Archie and Jughead . were drafted, faced down some antiwar protesters outside the induction center, and made clear their intentions to attend an upcoming peaceful protest march, all before being rejected as being underage. (The draft board had made a mistake.) In the intervening decades, Archie and his pals have dealt with the drug culture, pollution, war, inflation, and AIDS.*

Some of the effects of social change were handled more subtly. In the sixties "I Spy," the intrusion of the government into private lives is not the subject, but it is the reference point for Veronica's manipulations. And in "The Time of Your Life," also from the sixties, the youth culture issue—and the adult reaction to it—is universalized very effectively in what might well be called the Archie style.

Some of the changes in Archie *over the decades have been more than merely trendy. The addition of Chuck Clayton, a new black student at Riverdale High, and his girlfriend, Nancy, in the seventies was not merely politically and socially "correct," but necessary if* Archie *was to remain the idealized world of "average" American teenage life—as was the injection of Frankie Valdez, a new Hispanic student, and his girlfriend, Maria.*

Even more to the point was the issue in which Archie and Betty spend the night together in a terrible storm. Nothing happened, of course, but Betty's parents were sure of the worst. The implication was there, however, and the times had made it possible for Archie, *as in the forties, occasionally to play off the hidden tensions of teenage life to create memorable situations reminiscent of our own past.*

OPPOSITE, TOP TO BOTTOM: "Air Raid Warden," Archie #12 *(January–February 1945); from "Like Real Gone,"* Laugh #104 *(November 1959); from "New Look, Few Look,"* Betty and Veronica #39 *(November 1958); from "Fan Clubbed,"* Pals and Gals #6 *(1957–58); ABOVE, TOP TO BOTTOM: from "A Fool for Cool,"* The World of Archie #461 *(September 1977); from "Never Never Land,"* The World of Jughead #469 *(April 1978); from "The Time of Your Life,"* Betty and Veronica #156 *(December 1968)*

The Art of Archie

The *Archie* of Bob Montana and the wartime artists was a child of the original boom in comic books. Not only are the stories relatively more daring than those of later decades, they are more leisurely constructed and more graphically exciting. Though comic books are the children of the dailies, they are not simply longer versions of the comic strip. They are, in fact, a different form of sequential art.

As Joseph Witek has pointed out in *Comic Books as History,* comic books, which began life in the 1930s as anthologies of newspaper strips, "have evolved their own generic, narrative, and formal conventions." While both newspaper strips and comic books share "a common narrative vocabulary and grammar," they differ in their markets, in their cultural status, in their medium of presentation, and in the reading conventions they require.

Strips come unbidden, supplementary features of a newspaper, and their presentation is aesthetically arbitrary, imposed by the host medium, so that they are created under certain formal and thematic constraints. Strips have to be brief to fit copy requirements, and their themes have to be general and genteel enough for a broad "family" audience. Most of those that have survived are "gag" strips, three or four panels each day that end in a punch line. Even "continuity" strips— *Apartment 3-G, Mary Worth, Judge Parker*—have the slow pace and redundant narrative necessary to accommodate readers who look at the strip only occasionally.

Comic books are commodities in their own right, for sale to anyone, voluntary purchases. Especially today, with the development of what is called the *direct market* of comics specialty shops, comic books can come in all shapes and sizes with very few formal and thematic constraints. Major comic book publishers have produced commercially viable hardback and softcover books with individual circulations in the five-figure range.

Historically, the differences in market and medium have meant that comic strips are a socially acceptable form of sequential art, while comic books, in this country at least, are not. As an entertainment feature of newspapers, comic strips can be read by adults without social stigma, and as several of the studies point out in *Comics and Visual Culture,* the majority of newspaper comic strip readers are adults. Except for direct-market publications, which are directed at males between the ages of seventeen and thirty-five, comic books have been generally aimed at preteen, adolescent, and young-adult audiences. Consequently, the comic-book industry, like the motion picture, television, and popular recording industries, has suffered periodic conservative purges in which they are blamed for everything from eyeball mutilation to illiteracy.

Social and political implications aside, the markets and medium had from the start a tremendous impact on the formal development of comic *books* as distinct from *strips.* As the major newspapers continued to reduce the standard size of comic strips, meticulous visual detail and closely plotted action necessarily gave way to broad caricatures and mostly verbal humor. The ostensible narratives of continuity strips depended on the building up of incidents and the repetition of motifs rather than a sequence of events, and a Milton Caniff *Steve Canyon* adventure, for example (as opposed to, say, one from Caniff's old *Terry and the Pirates,* in which the hero actually grew up over time), would see its unaging hero drift into a new conflict as the current set of characters fell away. There was no sense of an ending, no dramatic climax, because the form only seldom permitted today's first panel to depend on the last panel of yesterday's sequence. Instead, it most often required repetition of needed information to understand the immediate action, a one-step backward for two-steps forward rhythm.

Comic books, by contrast, could do almost anything, the sizes and shapes of panels limited only by the artist's imagination and, perhaps, the 8½-by-11-inch page. Comic books worked in sequential segments, not just in a line of panels. The page, two-page spreads, and multipage, book-length, even multi-book-length stories constituted the structural units of a comic-book narrative. They could start with a full-page splash panel, a coherent single image establishing the theme and tone of the entire story, either summing up or initiating the action. Panels could be round or square or rectangular or nonexistent, depending on the rhythm of the story. They could be small to speed up the narrative, large to emphasize important moments of the action. They allowed for detailed exposition, complex visual and verbal effects, and a varied pace relying on visual space as well as narrative-reading time. Whereas a comic strip's unity is almost always visual—the reader sees the strip at once, including punchline—the comic book promises but constantly defers the ending till the final page and panel, allowing for such devices as foreshadowing and supporting the narrative drive that keeps readers reading. Veteran comic-book artist Will Eisner, creator of the elegant and famous *Spirit,* whose first comic-book work appeared in the 1936 publication *Wow, What A Magazine* issued by Henle Publishing Company, called this "reader discipline" —the artist's control of how a reader perceives the narrative structures of sequential art.

Consider, for example, the early, untitled *Archie* story in *Jackpot #4* (winter 1941), where Miss Grundy—still called "Mrs." at the time—appears in a single panel as Riverdale High's principal. The story opens with a full-page splash panel showing Archie directing a high-school class play while Betty plays an angel, whom Jughead, behind the curtain, hoists (above a dog sleeping onstage) by means of a rope tied around her waist. Inset at the bottom of the page are two small panels, one a circular overlay, the other the more typical carefully delineated rectangle. The page works as a piece—a tableau providing the setting and tone of the story and quickly establishing a relationship among the strip's three major characters. It also serves to kick off the slapstick action that follows in the story.

That action follows in two pages of standard comic-book form, three stacked columns of three panels each with only one circular panel to emphasize a change in visual perspective. On page one, Jughead lets go of the rope, Betty falls on Archie, and Archie now steps on the dog's tail, causing the animal to flee. We quickly learn that the play, which turns out to be *Uncle Tom's Cabin,* needs a bloodhound, and Archie hatches a scheme to find a new dog by raiding the dogcatcher's van. In doing so, Ar-

chie, Jughead, and Betty set loose a pack of hounds, and on page three we get a huge panel, two-thirds of a page in size, showing the effect of the freed hounds on the town. The panel culminates the opening action and seems to come right out of Hogan's Alley, with the same kind of visual and ethnic humor that made the Yellow Kid famous.

Afterward, the story returns to the auditorium and the play for new plot twists. Miss Grundy's appearance for one panel is purely and simply a visual joke, playing on the stereotype of the old maid as educator. The real adult foil in the story is Riverdale's mayor, who threatens on the last page to give Archie the tanning of his life.

The style and content of the humor, and a number of the visual elements, are still closely tied to the daily newspaper strips, but the nar-

rative itself and its unfolding over pages could only be accomplished in comic-book form. Montana would get much better at this art very quickly. By summer 1942, in the *Jackpot #6* story, which first developed the Reggie Mantle character (who had debuted in two panels of *Jackpot #5*), Montana illustrates his mastery of the medium, opening with an excellent splash panel (and it really is a *splash*) and using panel shapes and borders throughout to control the pace of his story and to create visually effective narrative connections.

After Montana left for the war, others followed in his footsteps. The *Archie* story in *Pep #54,* September 1945, called "This Teen Aged Steam Age," is almost free-form in its use of panel shapes and borders, while others tone down the variation by mixing Montana's comic-

Top: Splash panel from Jackpot #6 *(summer 1942), in which Reggie Mantle took an active role in an* Archie *story for the first time. Montana had created the prototype of Reggie in* Jackpot #5. Center: *from* Jackpot #4 *(winter 1941);* Bottom: *from "This Teen Aged Steam Age,"* Pep #54 *(September 1945). In 1945 the rail-riding bum was still very much a stock figure in popular entertainment. "This Teen Aged Steam Age" was only one of a number of* Archie *stories in the 1940s to include adult tramps. Once again playing off Archie's tenuous hold on things mechanical, the story is a good example of the freedom early comic-book artists felt in laying out their sequential images.*

book effects with more traditional daily strip techniques. Vigoda's "It's a Dog's Life," from *Laugh #27* of June 1948, and "Archie Gets the Bird," from *Archie #37* of March–April 1949, are good examples of his use of solid blacks and silhouettes.

After the mid-forties, the Archie stories in general, like all of those by Vigoda in particular, were strung on a strong narrative grid of two-panel tiers, three tiers to a page. Circular shapes and borderless panels were used for emotional emphasis within a single panel rather than to establish narrative rhythm or to create dramatic tension on the page itself.

In Vigoda's excellent "Car Trouble," from *Laugh #22,* spring 1947, the borderless panel just below the opening splash and the circular panels on the fourth, sixth, and eighth pages all serve as emotional close-ups—of Mr. Andrews's anger, of Archie's shock, of Mr. Andrews's anxiety, and of his surprise. Only the circular panels on the second page, shifting perspective on Archie's jalopy, the background circle on the eighth page, emphasizing the policeman's action in grabbing Mr. Andrews, and the threatening protrusion of the barber's razor-toting arm below the border of the right-hand top panel on top of the sixth page call to mind Montana's techniques, here used very conservatively. By September–October 1948, and *Archie #34,* we find in "The Hair Raiser" the narrative grid becoming almost rigid.

Despite the growing uniformity of the panel structure, much still depended on the individual artist. "The Battle of the Jitterbugs," in *Archie #30,* January–February 1948, is a classic example of a marriage between panel shape and narrative rhythm. The stronger grid could make "violating" it very effective indeed, as, for example, with the shapely legs in panels one and three on the second page of "Camera Bugs," from *Pep #48,* May 1948, a story that plays on the shortcomings of flat visuals without narrative context. And in the slightly earlier "No Body's Dummy," from *Pep*

#64, November 1947, a story many at Archie Comics think is the funniest story of the 1940s, the solid-black silhouettes play a critical narrative as well as compositional role.

In fact, the splash panel of "No Body's Dummy" is an excellent example of the codifying that was taking place in the late forties, not only of *Archie*'s visual vocabulary, but also of its narrative "grammar." In that panel, Veronica—leaning back, perched on a desk—says to Archie: "You always say you'd die for my sake, but you never do!" And Arch replies: "But you want me to be a—pin cushion in sewing class—what do you think I am, a dummy? (Don't answer that!)" And as a result of his use

of the word *dummy,* Archie decides to go find a real dummy, a manikin, to bring to Veronica and show her the difference. Never mind that it makes no sense, the point is that the almost ritualistic incantation of their relationship in the splash panel is the necessary starting point for an *Archie* adventure.

Not just the by-now-fixed relationships between the characters, but every aspect of Archie's world was taking on an iconographic cast. Never mind that in "The Old Home Town" Mr. Andrews is an office manager, and in "Talk of the Town" he is a real estate salesman. The point is the nostalgic "small-townness" of Riverdale itself. In the first story, the Andrewses decide not to move—despite the offer of a better job—when their neighbors and friends rally round for a farewell party. In the second, Archie and Jughead ruin Mr. Andrews's hopes of becoming rich when they foil a nefarious plan to buy up the town. Once the emotional connection between the characters and Riverdale was established, it would become a premise of the *Archie* narratives, just like Archie's worship of Veronica.

Here, too, we get an early example of a motif that was to become one of *Archie*'s most enduring features. Again and again over the next several decades, when the Archie "gang" is seriously threatened, all the fixed rivalries are forgotten, and the kids pull together for each other. Thus the "eternal" nature of adolescence, the seemingly never-ending relationships that a teenager can do nothing about, are given a positive turn. It is, in fact, this "cohesiveness" in real teenage life that lies behind the terrible loyalties of city gangs, but the Riverdale kids, despite the comic misery they cause each other, are an idealized gang whose bonding is totally positive.

Notice, too, that as the emotional quality of Riverdale is established in these stories, its geographic location becomes much less specific than in the earlier Montana stories. Ultimately, Riverdale itself would disappear into the scenes, props, and backdrops that wove the *Archie* series into a whole. Riverdale became a series of instantly recognizable props: Pop's Chocklit Shoppe, Riverdale High, Veronica Lodge's mansion, Archie's living room—no place but anyplace, the Hometown we love.

The disappearance of specificity, both in terms of place and characters, into a fixed, unvarying narrative routine was mirrored by the growing standardization of the narrative grid. It was precisely the lack of specificity that gave the *Archie* stories their universal appeal and effected the kind of nostalgic attraction to the series we discussed earlier. Some critics, like Stephen Becker, have attacked the *Archie* stories for being bland. That, in fact, is their strength. Others, like Witek, have labeled the process we are describing as a "denaturing." But that is how popular-culture icons work—emblematically, sans past, sans future, always current. An elderly Tarzan could not swing from the trees. A retired James Bond could not battle power-hungry madmen. So it is with Archie and his pals.

Not that the stories fail to reflect their times. In the 1940s, Archie and his pals jitterbug or help out air raid wardens; in the fifties they dress like beatniks; in the sixties they form a rock band; in the seventies they fight prejudice; in the eighties they help fight against drugs. *Archie* is really only a certain *kind* of story, a comic rendering of idealized teenage life. Its narrative appeal is timeless; the details of its telling, however, reflect the present.

By 1946, at least, the Archie formula was working so well that MLJ Comics gave up its superheroes to become Archie Comics. Each issue of an *Archie* comic book, whether it was *Pep,* or *Laugh,* or *Archie,* sold a million or so copies. By the late forties, *Archie* comics as a whole were the tenth-best-selling printed commodity in the world. Only the giants of publishing—such venerable magazines as *Time, Life, Look,* and the *Saturday Evening Post*—reached more readers.

The question of prejudice was raised in a quite familiar context in "A Matter of Prejudice," featuring Chuck Clayton, a black teenager who joined the Riverdale crowd in the 1970s. The story plays very cleverly with the notion that prejudice does not come automatically with skin-coloring, but is instead a question of preconceived ideas—specifically here, Archie's notions about Veronica's racism.

C'MON! LET'S MOVE FURTHER AWAY FROM "MY FRIENDS"! I MIGHT YELL JUST A BIT!

I'VE PUT UP WITH A LOT OF NONSENSE FROM YOU, VERONICA LODGE, AND ONLY BECAUSE I'M REAL GONE ON YOU!

BUT YOU'VE PUSHED ME TOO FAR THIS TIME! THE ONE THING I WON'T STAND FOR IS *PREJUDICE!*

NOW YOU CAN TAKE YOUR PARTY AND GO PLUMB TO BLAZES! --- *DIG?*

CHUCK CLAYTON IS *MY FRIEND*, BE HE GREEN, BLUE OR ORANGE! AND WHERE *I* GO, *HE* GOES! AND IF YOU DON'T *LIKE* IT, *LUMP IT!*

THAT DOES IT!

4.

UH- IT SEEMS THAT RON DOESN'T APPROVE OF *ALL* MY FRIENDS!

WHAT??

RANK PREJUDICE! WE'LL BOYCOTT THE PARTY! SHE CAN'T TREAT OUR PAL CHUCK THIS WAY!

A MATTER OF DRESS?

YEAH, CHUCK!

WE'D BETTER, GET IN TOUCH WITH EVERYONE SHE INVITED! CALL THEM ALL OFF! --- LET HER---

HEY! WHERE ARE YOU GUYS TAKING ME?

INTO YOUR OWN HOUSE, JUG!

ARRGH.!! NO.! IT'S UN-AMERICAN! I'VE GOTTA BE ME! I DON'T DRESS UP FOR *ANYBODY!*

VERONICA CAN'T HELP IT, PAL! SHE'S PREJUDICED!!

YEAH, AGAINST SLOBS!

The End

"Sugar Substitute," **Archie and Me #47** *(February 1972)*

THEY NEED A MAN'S EMOTIONAL STABILITY AND WISDOM!

WHAT'S THAT?

CRASH!

IT'S COMING FROM THE END CLASS ROOM!

KALUMP!

SEE? THAT'S A PERFECT EXAMPLE!

ONE OF THE WOMAN TEACHERS CAN'T MAINTAIN ORDER!

I'LL HAVE TO GO DOWN AND STRAIGHTEN THINGS OUT!

WELL, BELIEVE ME, I'LL GIVE HER A PIECE OF MY MIND!

I SUGGEST WE HAVE A SPECIAL WEEK FOR MR. WEATHERBEE!

THEY'RE GOING TO GET A SPECIAL WIG FOR YOU, SIR!

THAT'S THE LAST STRAW!

MISS BOING IS A REAL TROUBLE-MAKER!

I'M GOING IN THERE AND BUST THAT MEETING WIDE OPEN!

WOME LIB ME

LADIES, I'M SO PLEASED YOU AGREE WITH ME ABOUT WOMEN'S LIB!

IF WE TRY TO BE THE SAME AS MEN WE'LL TAKE A LOT OF THE *FUN* OUT OF LIFE!

I ENJOY HAVING MEN OPEN DOORS FOR ME!

10

"Commercial Conniption," Pep **#397** *(November 1984)*

WATCH THIS FLEA BRAIN DO *EXACTLY* WHAT MY TAPED COMMERCIAL TELLS HIM TO DO!

REACH OUT AND TOUCH SOMEONE!

REACH OUT AND TOUCH SOMEONE!

THE COMMERCIAL IS WORKING! OUR SUBJECT IS REACTING!

HA! HA! HE'S HEADING STRAIGHT FOR THAT PHONE BOOTH!

REACH OUT AND...

TELEPHON

??! HE'S PASSING THE PHONE BOOTH!

...*TOUCH SOMEONE!*

TELEPHONE

REGGIE, CAN I TOUCH YOU FOR A FIVE SPOT? I'LL PAY YOU BACK TOMORROW!

HE DIDN'T REACT *QUITE* LIKE WE EXPECTED!

OH, HE'S MERELY THE EXCEPTION THAT PROVES THE RULE!

2

THERE'S ANOTHER ONE!

I CAN'T BELIEVE WE'RE ACTUALLY LEAVING ON OUR VACATION!

DON'T LEAVE HOME WITHOUT THEM!

DON'T LEAVE HOME WITHOUT THEM!

MOM! DAD! WE'RE FORGETTING SOMETHING!

SEE! HE'S GOING BACK INSIDE TO GET THE FAMILY'S TRAVELLERS CHECKS!

WHEW! I ALMOST FORGOT MY LITTLE BLACK BOOK!

HOW COULD I CALL ALL MY GIRL FRIENDS WITHOUT IT?

GEE! THAT'S THE SECOND TEEN WHO'S LET US DOWN!

POOF! THEY ARE MERE STATISTICAL ERRORS!

Top row: **Archie's Christmas Love-in** *(January 1980);* **Jughead #334** *(June 1984);* **Everything's Archie #47** *(May 1976);* *Middle row:* **Veronica in Hawaii** *(December 1990);* **Pep #397** *(November 1984);* *Bottom row:* **Jughead #352** *(June 1986);* **Betty and Me #189** *(March 1991);* **Betty and Me #181** *(March 1990)*

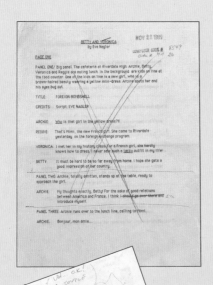

*A*rchie's *staff over the years has evidenced much of the stability and continuity that mark the stories themselves. Not only do the children and grandchildren of two of the founders—Louis Silberkleit and John Goldwater—run the company, but managing editor Victor Gorelick has been with Archie Comics some three decades. A former writer and colorist, Gorelick oversees a stable of writers and artists, many of whom—both staff and free-lance—have been with* Archie *as long as he has, or longer.*

Each story begins with a story idea. The Archie *writers submit their story ideas, sometimes complete story scripts, to Gorelick and the editorial staff each week. The story ideas sometimes come from young readers, but more often they are the results of conversations about current events, the news, popular trends, games, places of interest, and what stories have worked well in the past.*

Once the scripts have been written, submitted, revised, and accepted, they are assigned to one of Archie's *artists, many of whom are regular free-lancers, for penciling. The artist reads the script and, like a movie director, envisions the images and actions that will bring the script to life. The artist first lays out the page and lightly sketches the placement of backgrounds, figures, word balloons, and sound effects on 10-by-15-inch sheets of heavy paper. Satisfied with the layout, the "penciller" meticulously draws all the art in detail, erasing his layout sketch lines as he goes. When finished, he delivers the story-boards to Gorelick—by mail, messenger, or in person— for review.*

Gorelick approves the penciled art and sends them on to a "letterer," who letters in all the words, captions, story titles, and sound effects, using different-size pens and brushes. The letterer first creates guidelines in pencil, using a T-square and a letter-guide, to ensure uniform height and spacing for each letter and line, then letters the page. Next, the letterer inks in word balloons, thought balloons, or caption boxes that enclose the words. Sound effects, too, are inked in at this stage, as are all the panel lines that create the borders between images.

From there the story travels to the "inker," who completes the page by going over all the penciled art in black ink. As comic-book connoisseurs know, the final look of a page depends very much on the inker's skill, and the work of the original artist looks very different handled by different inkers.

With brushes and pens, thick and thin, with ruler, T-square, and triangle, all sporting raised edges, and with a pot of black india ink, the inker starts inking all the heads and human figures. Using a pen for small details—eyes, mouths, Archie's freckles—and a brush for outlining larger figures and filling in the solids, the inker works a page or two at a time to allow the ink to dry. Foregrounds get a heavier brush or pen line than backgrounds in order to create depth, and backgrounds are inked carefully, using usually a pen, the ruler, the T-square, and the triangle. Once completed, the inked pages are photocopied and sent off to the colorist.

Coloring is a vital part of comic-book art. From the simple use of green or red to convey the character's envy or anger through the use of light and dark to set the scene in day or night to the relative complexities of contrast, coloring not only supports the individual image but helps control the tempo of the story and in large measure provides its overall aesthetic tone. The colorist first takes the 10-by-15-inch inked pages and reduces them to actual comic size (today, 6 by 9 inches). The colorist then reads the story for specific references to color, before taking to the page with watercolors—which, more than any other medium, produce hues approximating those of printer's ink—and a soft red sable brush. Both the colored page and the original black-and-white artwork are sent to the printer.

This is the process, then, by which Archie's writers and artists have been producing their comic books for fifty years. Many of them—writers like Frank Doyle and George Gladir; artists (who also often doubled as writers) like George Frese, William Vigoda, Harry Lucey (all now deceased), and Stan Goldberg—were with Archie almost from the beginning. Others, too, especially contributed to Archie's development over the years: Joe Edwards, who drew the once quite popular L'il Jinx character; Sam Schwartz, whose specialty was Jughead (he was even often called "Jughead"); Bob Bolling, who created Little Archie; Dexter Taylor, who picked up where Bolling left off; Dan DeCarlo, who replaced Bob Montana as Archie's "premier" artist; letterer William Yoshida; inkers Rudy Lapick and John D'Agostino; colorist Barry Grossman; Digest editor Nanci Tsetsekas; and Rex Lindsey, Bill Golliher, and Dan Parent, relatively new additions to the stable, whose artwork is fast becoming the standard upon which Archie comics and licensed products are based.

An Island of Calm

The decade after World War II was the golden age of comic books. They cost a dime, they were sixty-four pages long, and—in a time before television—they provided cheap entertainment for a mass audience. But the very success of the new popular medium became one of its biggest problems. By the end of the war it was clear to many, not just those who read them, that comic books were a different animal entirely from the newspaper funnies.

If the differences in product and market afforded comic books a narrative and artistic range unavailable to daily strips, they also left comic books vulnerable to attack by mostly self-appointed guardians of public morality. In their day, comic strips, too, had suffered the disapprobation of contemporary arbiters of good taste and literary value, dismissed as lowbrow reading for the undoubtedly subliterate hoi polloi. But they were regulated by their host medium and never seriously challenged journalism's standards of propriety. The newspaper funnies had long been standard fare for virtually all families, an integral part of a daily publication that was an established American institution.

Comic books, independent publications that almost everyone, including kids, could afford, unlike almost all other media, had no one—neither advertisers, stockholders, nor a general public—to answer to for their quality or content. The comic book publisher was not a public figure with direct responsibility for his product; much of the time, no one was really sure *who* the publishers were. Add to that the fact that, from the beginning, comic books tapped into an imaginative vein that ran much closer to primal fears and desires than the newspaper strips, with few exceptions, ever did. More obviously then than now, when we have grown accustomed to them, the powerful fantasies embodied in Superman and Batman did indeed threaten the comfortable middle-class worldview exemplified by Dagwood Bumstead and, more recently, Charlie Brown. And as we have seen, even a series like *Archie,* a celebration of the commonplaces of middle-class youth, has a subconscious sensual core that creates its special vitality. All of this helps explain the virulent cultural hostility to comic books and why anticomic-book crusaders often bordered on hysteria in the charges they made.

The classic offender was E. C. Publications. "Educational Comics," founded by M. C. Gaines, the father of the comic-book form, published in the mid-forties a series of comic books called *Picture Stories,* which included comics on the Bible, American and world history, and science. These, however, could not compete successfully with the venerable *Classics Comics* and *Classics Illustrated,* and when Gaines failed in an effort to market his didactic product directly to elementary schools, E. C. Publications nearly went bust.

After Gaines died in 1947, his son William took over the company, changed the name to "Entertainment Comics," and launched a line of horror, science fiction, crime, and war comics that set the industry on its ear.

Only in the war genre did the didactic heart of the company beat on. Under the editorship of Harvey Kurtzman (who later would create E. C.'s most famous comic book, *Mad*), *Frontline Combat* and *Two-fisted Tales* featured stories based on historical fact and meticulously researched fictional pieces rich in period detail. Like all E. C. titles, they were sensational in their graphic presentation of organized death, managing at one and the same time to wallow in violence and convey a basically antiwar message, but their best pieces were committed to historical accuracy.

It was, however, such titles as *The Vault of Horror, Tales from the Crypt, Weird Science, Shock SuspenStories,* and *The Haunt of Fear* that earned E. C. an almost legendary notoriety. Under the banner of "New Trend" comics, E. C. transgressed just about every imaginable cultural taboo, producing "beautifully crafted, gleefully perverse" stories on incest, bondage, sadomasochism, dismemberment, disembowelment, and murders of all kinds, especially family murders. Cannibalism and necrophilia were such constant motifs that they became an E. C. hallmark.

The New Trend comics, and a whole spate of even more outrageous imitators, sparked a series of sociological studies of comic books by Gershon Legman, Frederic Wertham, and Geoffrey Wagner. All were uniformly negative, but of the three, Dr. Wertham's attack was probably the strongest. His book *Seduction of the Innocent* mobilized public indignation, focused the already extant social and governmental antagonism toward comic books, and spawned a congressional investigation and the threat of federal anticomic legislation.

In addition to the fumings of a few critics, certain social and economic changes were combining to rein in the excesses of comic books like those produced by E. C. The baby boom would vastly expand the potential comic-book audience, but that audience would be younger. And while juveniles have a fairly natural love of the sensational, parents tend to protect their preteen children from gore and sex. At the same time, the supermarket was coming into its own as a major outlet for comic books, and children purchasing books off the rack in plain view of their mother's grocery cart are limited in their choice of entertainment. The Comics Code Authority may historically have been a direct response to *Seduction of the Innocent,* but if there had been no Dr. Wertham, the industry would have had to invent him.

The Comics Code Authority was an independent board established in 1954 by the comic-book industry to review the editorial content of comic books. The Authority itself proclaimed the Code the "most stringent" in existence "for any communications media." The Code outlawed "displays of corrupt authority, successful crimes, happy criminals, the triumph of evil over good, violence, concealed weapons, the death of a policeman, sensual females, divorce, illicit sexual relationships, narcotics or drug addiction, physical afflictions, poor grammar, and the use of 'crime,' 'horror,' and 'terror' in the title of a magazine or story." The Code had to be strict, for the industry intended to use it to fight the very real threat of federal censorship; legislation was in fact pending when the Code was published, but it was subsequently opposed and defeated.

Dell Comics, one of the industry's major producers; the Gilberton Company, which published the *Classics Illustrated* series; and, of course, E. C. Comics refused to subscribe to the Code, all on the grounds that they had never published comic books that violated its tenets in the first place. While Dell and Gilberton published products that were both socially respectable and commercially viable, magazine distributors were leery of alienating parents and soon simply refused to handle most other non-Code-approved books. Dozens of small comic-book houses folded when they failed to replace their E. C. imitations with products of Dell's and Gilberton's quality and respectability. E. C. eventually lost most of its line, but survived by turning its flagship *Mad* into a black-and-white magazine, thereby evading the Code's strictures. By the late 1950s, few comics were sold anywhere in the country without the Authority's seal of approval.

The establishment of the Comics Code was probably the single most important event in the history of American comic books, and it was especially crucial to the development of Archie Comics. Archie's former president John Goldwater was one of the founders of the Comics Magazine Association of America and served as president of the CMAA for twenty-five years. And its present chairman, Michael Silberkleit, Louis Silberkleit's son, who joined the organization full-time in 1955, is currently president of the CMAA. Though Michael Silberkleit has helped to revise the Code, removing the most obdurate of its provisions, the Code still reflects the philosophy behind *Archie:* socially conservative, relentlessly wholesome, with a keen sense of moral responsibility, all solid suburban values for its solidly suburban audience.

The company itself is a family enterprise,

the home of three generations of Silberkleits and Goldwaters (Maurice Coyne left the company in the early seventies). In 1956, the year after Michael Silberkleit came on board, he was joined by the current president, Richard Goldwater, son of co-founder John Goldwater. Though the company went public in the seventies, the two sons took it private again to avoid a leveraged buy-out in January 1983. In 1984, David Silberkleit, Michael's son, became part of the firm. He is now vice president in charge of marketing. In 1985, Richard Goldwater's daughter, Lisa, became an *Archie* editor.

These are all people who grew up with Archie and his pals. Michael Silberkleit, who runs the business, and Richard Goldwater, who handles editorial, worked at part-time jobs for the company as teenagers and during summers in college. Both of them hawked *Archie* comic books at New York's Grand Central Terminal to the crowds of summer-camp kids. Such continuity extends beyond the immediate family members. Managing editor Victor Gorelick has been with the firm some three decades, working his way up after coming to *Archie* as an artist just out of high school. Several of the writers and artists in his stable have been working on the Riverdale High gang at least as long as Gorelick, some longer. The people at *Archie* seem acutely aware that they are husbanding what is in effect an American institution. Gorelick and Michael Silberkleit both talk about *Archie* as an island of calm in the stormy seas of their preteen readers' lives. As they see it, in a society plagued by drugs, violence, and broken homes, *Archie*'s idealized Riverdale offers them a legitimate avenue of escape to the world as they would like it to be, where parents never divorce and teenagers are important. It's a sort of reverse nostalgia, realistic enough for the readers to identify with the characters and their problems, but stylized enough to be funny and entertaining. And that, precisely, was the rationale behind the Comics Code: to protect young readers from the graphic

portrayal of violence and perversion.

The average reader of *Archie* is today, and probably has been since the fifties, an eleven-year-old female. The *Archie* that she knows came into final focus with the establishment of the Code. It is important to remember how truly odd a comic-book character Archie was in the early fifties. Not nearly so realistically drawn as the E. C. New Trend characters or the muscle-bound superheroes, the *Archie* populace had common, down-to-earth problems in an everyday world. In that sense, *Archie* was perhaps the only, certainly the most prominent, realistic comic book.

The effect of the Comics Code was to make *Archie* the standard, rather than the exception, in comic books. The New Trend style of comics simply disappeared, and the superheroes suffered a major decline. Only at DC Comics, the home of Superman and Batman, did they live on, though more overtly fantastic than ever before, with their villains who couldn't triumph or be happy in their evil even for a moment; with their policemen who couldn't die; and with their figures of authority who were never wrong. Not until the Marvel superheroes of the mid-sixties would moral ambiguity return to mainstream comics. And not until the underground "comix" of the later sixties would E. C.'s latent heritage of rebellion against the dominant culture come to fruition.

By contrast, *Archie* thrived. The trend toward a standardized narrative grid continued as the sexual basis of the central relationships became even more repressed. Betty and Veronica became a bit more cartoony, with no longer even a hint that they might be "sensual females," which the Code expressly forbade. But such restrictions actually worked in favor of the *Archie* series. The more visceral realities of teenage life became totally latent in the *Archie* narratives, hidden in the less threatening concept, say, of being "boy crazy." Similarly, the intense bonding of teenage life, born from the explosion of hormones that make it so volatile, became a source of wholesome solidarity for the Riverdale adolescents. At a time in the fifties, when the phenomenon of urban teenage gangs filled with "juvenile delinquents" was a hot new topic in the popular press, in fiction and film, and in sociological treatises, Archie and his pals provided a model "antigang."

In short, *Archie* tamed teenage life, not evading its very real problems, but presenting them in a form that a preteen could handle.

Take Big Moose's overprotection of "his girl" Midge. In real life, such violence and obsessiveness would surely indicate a sexual attachment. In *Archie,* Moose's jealous poundings are simply the premise of the narrative action in such stories as "Call to Arms," from *Archie #86,* May–June 1957. The preteen can read the story, identify with it, perhaps laugh at it, and learn from it, without having to struggle with the sexual issue directly. Also, we see in this story the kind of idealization of the typical teenager's intense bonding we have been discussing. Moose (temporarily) changes his ways and allows Archie to take Midge out on a Saturday night because he believes that his jealous rage actually hurt Archie earlier in the story, and that is something no Riverdale kid, not even Moose, would ever do intentionally.

If *Archie* was safe because it was idealized, it also captured something of the "feeling" of teenage life in its comic book form, with its never-aging characters and always given situations and relationships. Which is why reading *Archie* still evokes the memory of adolescence for the adult. As adults, for example, we may have grown interested in Veronica's emotional attachment to her father for what it suggests about the psychological depth of feeling between father and daughter. As young readers, however, we understood it simply as part of the story, a given, not to be pondered, but to be enjoyed for where it leads the action. As kids, we saw in *Archie* a hundred variations on the classic panel of Veronica, her eyes closed, her

face set in outrage, the word balloon above her head shouting "DADDY!" We did not give it a second thought. For the adult, the image so perfectly defines Veronica as to be a work of art: We understand everything about her when we see it, and we remember when we did not understand—just as we do about our own past.

It was such codified images and the standardized narratives they engendered, then, that made Archie and his pals the prototypes of American teenage life. The material of *Archie* was to prove amazingly resilient. Even popular music, a mainstay of teenage rebellion, could not resist its power. When the Riverdale kids formed The Archies band, sex, drugs, even rock 'n' roll disappeared into the sweet, wholesome sounds of bubble-gum music as "Sugar, Sugar" hit the top of the charts. Through the decades, the *Archie* artists carefully studied the trends in clothing and the fads in language and leisure of American youth and faithfully reproduced them. One can almost guess the era of a given story by skirt lengths, hair styles, and the vocabulary of the word balloons. The characters and their relationships proved so stable that they could translate into other media: a radio show during the forties, a run of successful Saturday morning television cartoons in the late 1960s, 1970s, and 1980s.

Even when the social upheavals of the sixties loosened the hold of the Code, and the development of the direct market all but de-

stroyed it, *Archie* remained *Archie* and still flourished. More socially conscious themes appeared, especially in the seventies, and in the eighties *Archie* has dealt with such controversial subjects as drug addiction and AIDS. In the nineties, a number of stories dealt with environmental issues. Of this, the people at *Archie* are justly proud. And, recently, Moose has turned out to be not the big, stupid lug we all thought he was, but instead a kid suffering from dyslexia. Unlike Superman and Batman, however, who these days have returned with a vengeance to the violence that would put even the New Trend comics to shame in such direct market titles as *The Dark Knight Returns* and *The Man of Steel, Archie* continues to be resolutely mainstream. One of the best measures of the strength of the core characters in *Archie* are the sales figures—today somewhere in the range of 16.5 million comic books annually. Even more to the point, whereas DC Comics or Marvel might outsell *Archie* overall, they do it with a wide range of characters in a variety of genres. *Archie*'s sales (from *Everything's Archie* to *Riverdale High,* some forty-one in all) depend entirely on the same small group of characters.

When the Comics Code gave final shape to the tenor of the Archie narratives over three decades ago, *Archie* became not just the most appropriate kind of story for a mainstream comic-book audience, it also became the official version of middle-class teenage life. And it has remained so ever since. That is the reason why a preteen can find in *Archie* a reassuring glimpse into her or his near future, while older readers like ourselves see our own past. For Archie and Jughead, Betty and Veronica, Reggie, Moose, Midge, and the others have defined for half a century what it means to be seventeen-going-on-eighteen in America.

TOP: *In the 1950s, Archie as a character developed some smarts he quite lacked in the previous decade. Still girl-crazy, still capable of making a complete fool of himself when it came to Veronica and Betty, still able unwittingly to send adults like Mr. Weatherbee, Mr. Lodge, and his own father into orbit, he yet seemed*

much less a klutz, more often in control of the situation, as in "Call to Arms," from Archie *#86 (May–June 1957).* ABOVE: *T-shirt featuring Veronica in a typical moment.*